THE BOOK OF 1930's BRITISH MOTORCYCLE CARBURETTERS AND ELECTRICAL COMPONENTS

Carburetters:
- AMAC
- AMAL
- BINKS
- VILLIERS

Electrical Components:
- B.T.H.
- LUCAS
- MILLER
- VILLIERS

A Floyd Clymer 'Motorcyclist's Library' publication
Published in 2018 by: www.VelocePress.com

All rights reserved. This work may not be reproduced or transmitted in any form without the express written consent of the publisher. © 2018 Veloce Enterprises Inc.
San Antonio, Texas, U.S.A.

INTRODUCTION

Welcome to the world of digital publishing ~ the book you now hold in your hand, was printed using the latest state of the art digital technology. The advent of print-on-demand has forever changed the publishing process, never has information been so accessible and it is our hope that this book serves your informational needs for years to come. If this is your first exposure to digital publishing, we hope that you are pleased with the results. Many more titles of interest to the classic automobile and motorcycle enthusiast, collector and restorer are available via our website at www.VelocePress.com. We hope that you find this title as interesting as we do.

NOTE FROM THE PUBLISHER

The information presented is true and complete to the best of our knowledge. All recommendations are made without any guarantees on the part of the author or the publisher, who also disclaim all liability incurred with the use of this information.

TRADEMARKS

We recognize that some words, model names and designations, for example, mentioned herein are the property of the trademark holder. We use them for identification purposes only. This is not an official publication.

INFORMATION ON THE USE OF THIS PUBLICATION

This manual is an invaluable resource for those interested in performing their own maintenance. However, in today's information age we are constantly subject to changes in common practice, new technology, availability of improved materials and increased awareness of chemical toxicity. As such, it is advised that the user consult with an experienced professional prior to undertaking any procedure described herein. While every care has been taken to ensure correctness of information, it is obviously not possible to guarantee complete freedom from errors or omissions or to accept liability arising from such errors or omissions. Therefore, any individual that uses the information contained within, or elects to perform or participate in do-it-yourself repairs or modifications acknowledges that there is a risk factor involved and that the publisher or its associates cannot be held responsible for personal injury or property damage resulting from the use of the information or the outcome of such procedures.

WARNING!

One final word of advice, this publication is intended to be used as a reference guide, and when in doubt the reader should consult with a qualified technician.

THE BOOK OF 1930's BRITISH MOTORCYCLE CARBURETTERS AND ELECTRICAL COMPONENTS

CONTENTS

Subject	Page

CARBURETTERS (by Manufacturer & Type)

AMAC: E & H.	1
AMAL: 4, 5, 6, 26, 27 & 29.	3
BINKS: 46, 47, 48, 49, LR & 3 Jet version for Scott Motorcycles.	20
VILLIERS: Single & Double Lever.	27

ELECTRICAL COMPONENTS (by Manufacturer & Type – where appropriate)

IGNITION: Theory.	31
MAGNETOS: BTH K1, K2 & M2.- Lucas M-L - Villiers Flywheel Magneto.*	35
SPARKING PLUGS: Maintenance, repairs & adjustments.	65
BATTERIES & CABLES: Maintenance & repairs.*	73
LAMPS, SWITCHES & INSTRUMENTS: BTH, Miller, Lucas & Villiers.*	84
DYNAMOS, CUT OUTS & REGULATORS: Direct Current Dynamos, DC Magneto Dynamos, DC Coil Ignition Dynamos, AC Flywheel lighting & ignition units, AC Mag-generators, Cut outs & Regulators.*	97

* Includes a 'Faults and Remedies' section.

The predominance of the data included in this publication was compiled from 1924-1932 service documentation. However, much of that same information is applicable to motorcycles manufactured before and after those dates.

This publication also includes a complete listing of titles in the 'Motorcyclist's Library' series. Many of those books expand on the repair and maintenance procedures for other mechanical and electrical components and will be of assistance to owners and restorers of classic, vintage and veteran motorcycles.

TYPES OF MOTOR-CYCLE CARBURETTERS

By E. W. KNOTT, M.I.A.E.

AMONGST the best-known names are Amac, Brown & Barlow, Binks, Senspray, Schebler, Villiers, Bowden and Capac. In addition one or two motor-cycle manufacturers made their own carburetters, such as B.S.A. and Triumph. At the end of 1927 an amalgamation took place between Amac, Brown & Barlow and Binks in which technical and other resources were pooled under the title of Amalgamated Carburetters Ltd., their products being known as Amal Carburetters.

In view of the vast number of the older types of Amac and Brown & Barlow carburetters still in use, these will be dealt with, as well as the latest Amal models.

THE AMAC CARBURETTER

Manufacturers: AMALGAMATED CARBURETTERS, LTD., Holford Works, Perry Barr, Birmingham. Telephone: Birmingham East 1371-2-3-4-5. Telegrams: Amalcarb Phone, Birmingham.

Sports Type with " E " Type Sprayer

The general layout of this carburetter will be seen in Fig. 1. The float chamber is of the bottom feed type and can be removed by unscrewing the jet holder, when a slight twist will free it. No fibre washers are used for the float-chamber joint as in later models, coned metal-to-metal faces being employed. When reassembling the float chamber to the mixing chamber, care must be taken to see that all traces of grit, etc., are removed from these faces, or leakage will take place and possibly the joint be permanently damaged.

How to tune an Amac Carburetter

This is extremely simple, and consists mainly of choosing the correct size jet. The best indication of this is the amount which the air lever can be opened, and if the latter can be moved to three-quarter open position when running at full speed, the jet is of correct size.

Special Setting for Double Lever Type " H " (1920) and for Type " E " (1914-19) Carburetters

When finding the correct setting for these carburetters never use a jet that allows both the throttle and air levers to be fully opened at the same

TYPES OF MOTOR-CYCLE CARBURETTERS

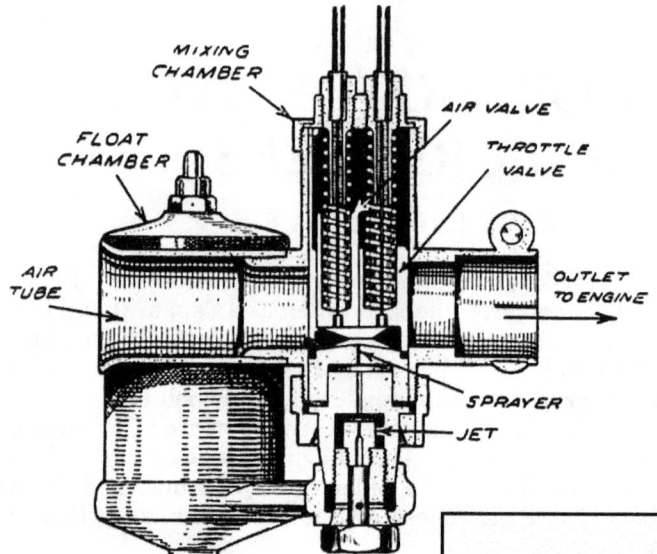

Fig. 1.—Sports Type Amac Carburetter with "E" Type Sprayer.

time. The area through the mixing chamber is greater than that of the induction pipe stump on which the carburetter fixes, which means that no benefit will be obtained by drilling out or filing the spraying chamber in an endeavour to admit more air to the engine. For ordinary touring work, if the air lever can be opened from two-thirds to three-quarters when the engine is going all out with fully opened throttle, the jet has been correctly chosen. Should it not be found possible to open the air lever this amount, the jet is too small. On the contrary, if it can be opened more than this amount, the jet is too large.

These carburetters are semi-automatic in action, and the throttle lever can be moved through a fairly wide range, once the engine is warmed up, without having to alter the air lever. The air lever should be closed for starting and slow running and also closed somewhat when climbing steep hills.

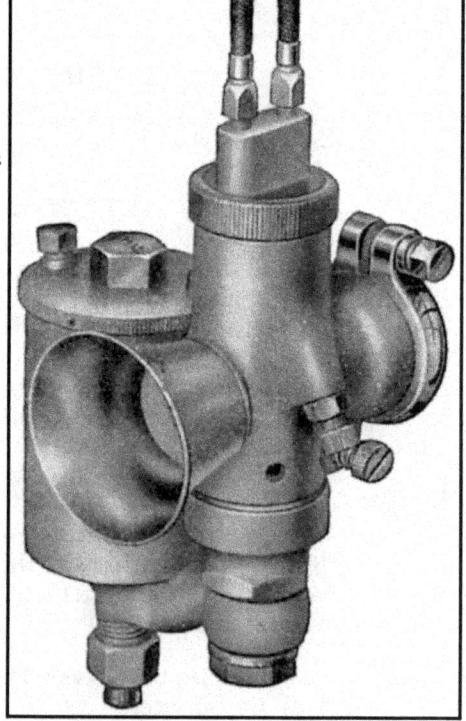

Fig. 2.—The 1930-1 Amal Carburetter, showing Throttle Stop and Pilot Air Screw.

TYPES OF MOTOR-CYCLE CARBURETTERS

Jet Sizes
There is a tendency on the part of most riders to fit a jet larger than necessary, the fact that the suction on the jet can be increased by closing the air lever being ignored.

Throttles
There are three shapes of throttle valve made, Nos. 2 and 3 being most commonly used. For two-stroke engines in give-and-take country No. 3 is best, but in hilly districts a No. 2 valve should be fitted, as it helps to sustain power on hills.

THE AMAL CARBURETTER FOR 1930-1
General Fitting Instructions
This carburetter is fitted with a needle-controlled main jet and is very similar to their 1928 type. The table on page 4 gives the standard setting for single-cylinder engines of the four-stroke type. A further table for track racing is given later.

Setting for Alcohol Fuels
For alcohol fuels on the standard Amal carburetter a ·113 needle jet must be fitted, together with No. 3 cut-away throttle valve. The taper needle must also be raised to the fourth position for P.M.S.2 and the fifth position for R.D.1. The pilot air-adjusting screw should be closed off in each case. Also the following increase in the main jets must be made:

Size of petrol and petrol-benzole jets in c.c.	Size of jet for P.M.S.2 and R.D.2	Size of jet for R.D.1	Size of petrol and petrol-benzole jets in c.c.	Size of jet for P.M.S.2 and R.D.2	Size of jet for R.D.1
25	40	45	140	220	260
30	45	55	160	260	300
35	55	65	180	280	325
40	60	75	200	300	375
50	80	90	220	350	400
60	95	110	240	375	450
70	110	130	260	400	475
80	120	150	280	450	525
90	140	170	300	475	550
100	160	180	325	500	600
120	180	220	350	550	650

The present method of marking Amal jets differs from that used with their earlier types. For a table showing comparative sizes and markings see page 4.

Having chosen a carburetter with the appropriate setting, the following details in fitting must be observed if the carburetter is to function properly. See that the carburetter is firmly fixed with an airtight joint

TYPES OF MOTOR-CYCLE CARBURETTERS

AMAL CARBURETTERS, 1930-1

STANDARD SETTINGS, FOUR-STROKE SINGLE-CYLINDER ENGINES

Setting for Petrol, Benzole, Petrol-Benzole Mixtures and Ethyl Petrol

Engine	Carb. type No.	Bore size No.	Jet	Needle position	Model valve
50–75 c.c.	—	—	—	—	—
75 to 100 c.c.	—	—	—	—	—
100 to 125 c.c.	—	—	—	—	—
150 to 175 c.c.	—	—	—	—	—
175 c.c.—					
S.V. Touring	4	17A	60	3	4/5
O.H.V. Touring	4	17A	60	3	4/5
O.H.V. Sports	4	21A	70	3	4/5
O.H.V. Racing	4	25A	90	3	4/4
250 c.c.—					
S.V. Touring	4	21A	70	3	4/5
O.H.V. Touring	4	25A	80	3	4/5
O.H.V. Sports	4	25A	80	3	4/5
O.H.V. Racing	5	28A	100	3	4/4
O.H.V. Racing	5	33A	120	3	4/4
300 c.c.—					
S.V. Touring	4	21A	70	3	4/5
350 c.c.—					
S.V. Touring	4	25A	80	3	4/5
O.H.V. Touring	4	25A	80	3	4/5
O.H.V. Touring	5	28A	95	3	5/5
O.H.V. Sports	5	33A	110	3	5/5
O.H.V. Sports	6	39A	130	3	6/5
O.H.V. Racing	6	45A	160	3	6/4
500 c.c.—					
S.V. Touring	5	33A	110	3	5/5
S.V. Touring	6	39A	130	3	6/5
O.H.V. Touring	6	45A	140	3	6/5
O.H.V. Sports	6	45A	140	3	6/5
O.H.V. Sports	6	51A	160	3	6/5
O.H.V. Racing	6	51A	180	3	6/4
O.H.V. Racing	29	54A	200	3	29/4
600 c.c.—					
S.V. Touring	6	39A	130	3	6/5
S.V. Touring	6	45A	140	3	6/5
O.H.V. Touring	6	45A	140	3	6/5
O.H.V. Sports	6	51A	160	3	6/4
O.H.V. Racing	29	58A	200	3	29/4
O.H.V. Racing	29	65A	220	3	29/4

NOTE.—Racing refers to road racing; for track racing settings, see page 15. For multi-cylinder engines take the capacity of one cylinder only to select carburetter and use a throttle valve with one cut-away smaller.

to the engine, and that the float chamber is in an upright position. A free flow of petrol must be ensured by having a pipe of at least $\frac{3}{16}$ inch inside bore, the pipe being free from kinks or bends where air can be trapped. For racing purposes $\frac{1}{4}$-inch bore pipe should be used.

TYPES OF MOTOR-CYCLE CARBURETTERS

Before attempting to adjust the length of the cables, the control levers must be fixed in position and the casings clipped to the frame, as unless this is done the adjustment will alter as the casing moves. Backlash can then be taken out of the cables by turning the knurled adjusting screws on top of the mixing chamber where the casing enters. If it is found that with the throttle control lever in the " closed " position the throttle refuses to shut in spite of correct adjustment of the length of its casing, slack off the throttle stop screw until the throttle closes sufficiently and relock the screw with the nut provided.

Testing for Correct Main Jet Size

The jet sizes given in the table (page 4) will suit all ordinary conditions, but peculiarities in engine design, climatic conditions, etc., may call for some slight alteration, and a check may be made as follows. Set the air lever three-quarters of the way open and try for the jet size that gives maximum power and speed with full-open throttle. This size of jet will give the best all-round performance, but if maximum power and speed are all that matter, test with the air slide fully open.

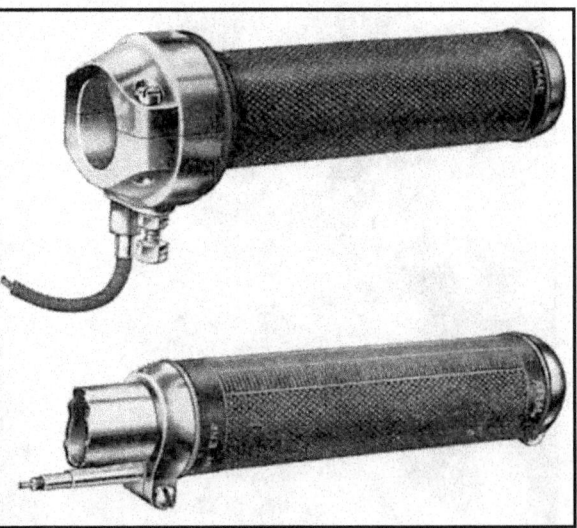

Fig. 3.—(*Above*) THE BINKS TWIST-GRIP CONTROL.
(*Below*) THE AMAL TWIST-GRIP CONTROL.

At ordinary cruising speeds the jet size can be checked by slightly closing and opening the air lever. If when gradually closing the lever there is an increase in speed, it is an indication that the jet is on the small side. On the other hand, if the speed increases when the air slide is moved to the full-open position, the jet is slightly too large for ordinary touring conditions.

Slow Running

The next procedure is to set the throttle stop for slow running. Reference has already been made to the importance of correctly adjusting the control cables, and assuming this has been done and the engine warmed up, the throttle stop screw can be slowly screwed in or out until the engine ticks over at a satisfactory speed with the control lever in the " closed " position. If during this adjustment the engine begins to miss,

TYPES OF MOTOR-CYCLE CARBURETTERS

or fire erratically, the pilot air-adjusting screw should be turned one way or the other until the engine beat becomes even and clean.

THE 1930-1 AMAL CARBURETTER, TYPES 4, 5 AND 6

These instruments are a combination of the Amac and Brown & Barlow carburetters, special care having been given to the shape of the intake passage throughout so as to give the maximum possible freedom for the air on its way through. The proportion of air to petrol in these models is controlled by means of a tapered needle which moves up and down with the throttle, means being provided to alter the position of the needle relative to the throttle.

A fixed jet is used to limit the amount of fuel passing to the engine at full-open throttle, whilst idling is definitely controlled by means of a pilot jet with air adjustment as well as a throttle stop screw.

Controls

These carburetters are supplied both with double and single levers, the latter having a hand-operated air valve for starting purposes. The twist-grip type of control is also very popular. The two best known are the Amal and the Binks, the latter being specially recommended for fast touring and racing owing to its quick action. Figs. 5 and 6 show the method of removing the control wire from the Amal model.

Fig. 4.—Setting the Throttle Stop on the Amal Carburetter.

TYPES OF MOTOR-CYCLE CARBURETTERS

Constructional Details of the Amal Carburetter (1930)

Referring to the lettered diagram, Fig. 7, the body or mixing chamber A has located in its upper part the throttle valve B which carries in it

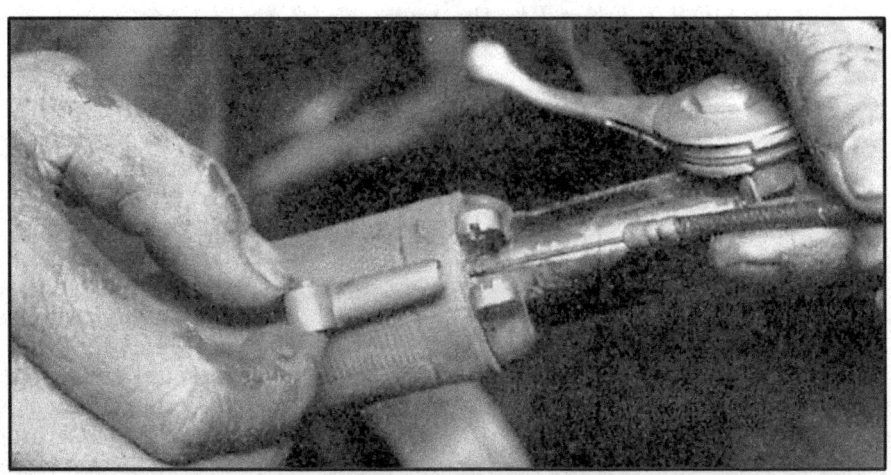

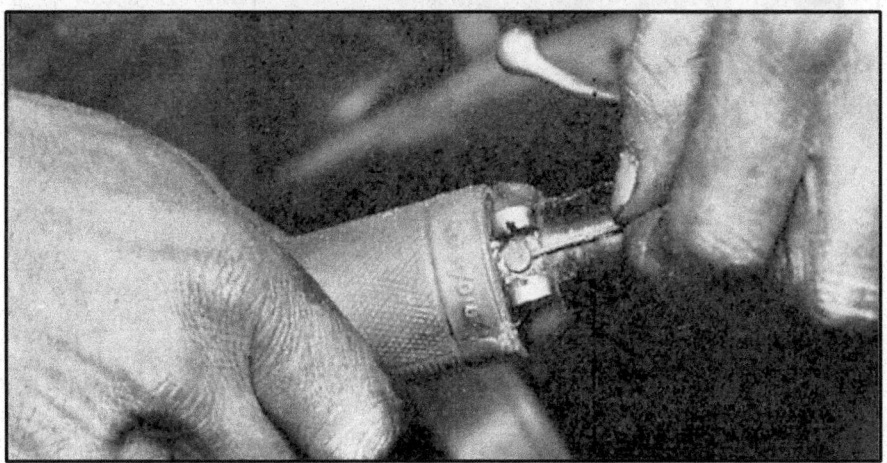

Figs. 5 and 6.—REMOVING CABLE FROM AMAL TWIST-GRIP CONTROL.

The outer casing is pulled back, allowing the slotted distance piece to be lifted out; note the two slots in the clip with which this registers; then rotate the grip as though closing, which will expose the nipple, thus allowing the cable to be disengaged.

the taper needle C which can be fixed in any one of five positions by pulling out the clip, moving the needle upwards or downwards to the desired position and refixing by pressing the needle clip back into position.

TYPES OF MOTOR-CYCLE CARBURETTERS

In a recess in the throttle valve will be found the brass air valve D, the up-and-down movement of which is controlled by the air-valve lever and which is used to regulate the petrol-air mixture by varying the suction on the jet. The smaller the opening, the fiercer the suction and vice versa.

The jet block F is fixed to the underside of the mixing chamber by the union nut E, a fibre washer, which on no account must be omitted when reassembling the carburetter, ensuring a petrol-tight joint. The jet block is located in its correct position by a small pin which fits in a slot cut out of the threaded portion of the mixing chamber on which the union nut E screws. The adapter body H forms the upper part of the jet block, whilst in the lower part will be found the small hole forming the pilot jet J which is fed directly from the float chamber via the passage K.

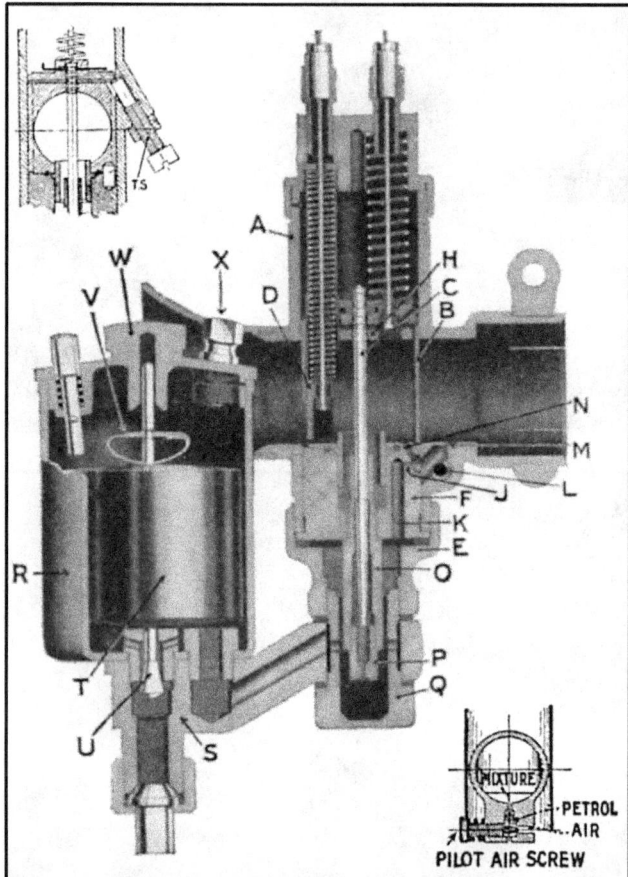

Fig. 7.—A Section through the Amal Carburetter, showing also the Action of the Throttle Stop and the Pilot Air Screw.

Across the bottom of the mixing chamber is drilled a passage L, one end of which leads to the air outside the carburetter, the other being fitted with a spring-loaded screw known as the pilot air screw. The amount of air entering the passage can be varied by moving this screw in or out, the air diluting the mixture issuing from the pilot outlet M and the bypass N. The pilot outlet is on the engine side of the throttle in the mixing chamber, whilst the bypass outlet is in the jet block F, just inside the wall of the mixing chamber in which the throttle slides.

Removal of the jet plug Q and the float chamber discloses the needle

TYPES OF MOTOR-CYCLE CARBURETTERS

jet O, in the bottom of which is screwed the main jet P. Both of these jets can be easily unscrewed by means of a small adjustable spanner.

Float Chamber

This consists of the container R mounted on the platform S. The cover W screws into the top, and in the case of the large size float chamber is fitted with a locking screw X, which pulls the rim of the cover hard down on to the top edge of the container R. Passing up the centre of the float chamber is the needle valve U, which is lifted by the float T. One end of the needle valve is tapered to form a petrol-tight joint in the needle valve seat, which is situated either in the bottom of the float chamber or else in the cover, depending on the type of float chamber, i.e. bottom feed or top feed. A clip fixes the float on the needle in a manner which enables it to be easily removed for cleaning purposes or renewal.

The edge of the cover is knurled for ease of turning by hand and a hexagon in the centre enables it to be firmly tightened by means of a suitable spanner. When using this spanner care must be taken not to bend the small projecting knob used for "flooding" the carburetter when starting from cold; if it should become bent it may stick

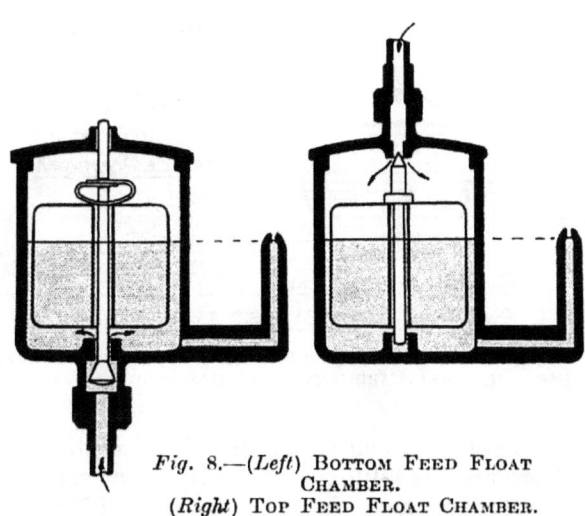

Fig. 8.—(*Left*) BOTTOM FEED FLOAT CHAMBER.
(*Right*) TOP FEED FLOAT CHAMBER.

down permanently, causing the carburetter to flood continuously. The weight of the float and the position of the groove on the needle are carefully fixed to ensure the correct level of fuel in the float chamber, and any departure from the makers' setting will either cause fuel starvation or flooding.

Operation of the Amal Carburetter

Having turned on the petrol and allowed the float chamber to fill to its correct level, the throttle valve should be only slightly opened. As the kick-starter is operated and the piston in the engine descends on the induction stroke, a powerful suction is created on the engine side of the throttle, causing air to rush in through the pilot air hole L taking petrol with it from the pilot jet J. This mixture of air and petrol passes to the

TYPES OF MOTOR-CYCLE CARBURETTERS

engine via the outlet hole M. This mixture is extremely rich, but the passage is insufficiently large to pass enough mixture to " idle " the engine so that it is necessary to open the throttle to pass additional air from the main air intake. The exact amount of throttle opening for this purpose can be minutely regulated by means of the throttle stop screw.

Opening up the throttle valve still more will reduce the suction on the outlet M but will correspondingly increase the suction on the bypass outlet N so that mixture will issue from both openings. At approximately one-eighth throttle opening fuel begins to issue from the main jet system. From one-eighth to one-quarter opening the mixture control depends on what is known as throttle-valve cut away, the exact meaning of which is given in the paragraph devoted to this detail.

From one-quarter to three-quarters open throttle the mixture is controlled by the position of the needle C and from thereon until full throttle the main jet alone controls the mixture. By closing the air valve D, thereby reducing the free passage of air through the mixing chamber, the suction on the main jet can be increased with a consequent enriching of the mixture.

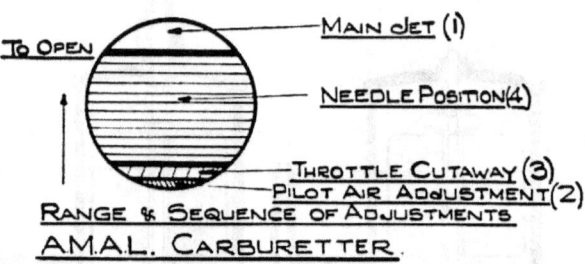

Fig. 9.—THE RANGE AND SEQUENCE OF ADJUSTMENTS OF THE AMAL CARBURETTER SHOWN DIAGRAMMATICALLY.

How to tune a 1930-1 Amal Carburetter

It is important that a definite routine should be observed when tuning the Amal carburetter (in fact all carburetters). Here are the adjustments in their correct order.

(1) The main jet, the influence of which is most definite between three-quarters and full throttle.

(2) The air adjustment to the pilot jet affecting the closed to one-eighth throttle opening.

(3) The amount of the throttle valve cut away on the air intake side, which controls the mixture from one-eighth to one-quarter throttle opening.

(4) The height at which the needle is set relative to the throttle valve. Fig. 9 shows diagrammatically these separate phases and their sequence of operation.

(a) **Size of Main Jet**

Reference to the table on page 4 will enable the reader to choose very closely the size of main jet required for any particular type of engine, the method of checking the exact size having already been dealt with.

TYPES OF MOTOR-CYCLE CARBURETTERS

(b) **Adjustment of Pilot Jet**

Turning the screw to the right or in a clockwise direction cuts off some of the air and thereby enriches the idling mixture. Turning the screw to the left, or anticlockwise, weakens the idling mixture.

Starting up before Carburetter is Properly Tuned.—Set the air-adjusting screw to the pilot jet as far in as possible, open throttle about one-eighth, press down the tickler for three or four seconds and start up engine. Allow to warm up and gradually close throttle. The slow-running mixture will be naturally very rich (owing to the pilot air-adjusting needle being screwed home) and the needle should require to be unscrewed to obtain steady idling. If this is not the case, air is entering the induction system somewhere between the throttle and the cylinder head, and search should be made for air leaks. Badly worn inlet-valve guides can also cause this. By adjusting both throttle stop screw and pilot air screw the engine should be made to tick over smoothly and slowly. Only in those instances where the rider wishes to stop the engine by closing the throttle should the throttle stop screw be screwed out sufficiently far to allow complete closing of the throttle, but the throttle stop screw should never be removed altogether and the lock nut must always be securely tightened.

Causes of Bad Idling.—Air leaks at the point where carburetter joins engine.

Worn inlet valve stem or guide.
Too much advance of magneto.
Bad sparking plugs or plugs with too small a gap.
Dirty contact breaker.
Oil on slip ring.
Short on high-tension cable to frame.
Other ignition faults.

(c) **Throttle Valve Cut Away**

Having obtained the best possible idling, put air lever wide open and set ignition at half advance. Next open the throttle very slowly and observe whether the engine picks up steadily or whether the engine staggers. If spitting back takes place through the carburetter the mixture is too weak, whilst if black smoke is ejected from the exhaust pipe and the engine runs in a lumpy fashion, the mixture is too rich. These symptoms decide the shape of the throttle cut away. If there are signs of weak mixture a throttle valve with *less* cut away should be fitted, whilst if richness is evident, a *larger* cut away is called for.

Identification Marks of Throttle Cut Away.—Every Amal throttle valve has two numbers stamped on it, the first giving the type number of the carburetter and the second the amount of cut away measured in sixteenths of an inch. For example, a valve stamped 6/4 would mean that it was a

TYPES OF MOTOR-CYCLE CARBURETTERS

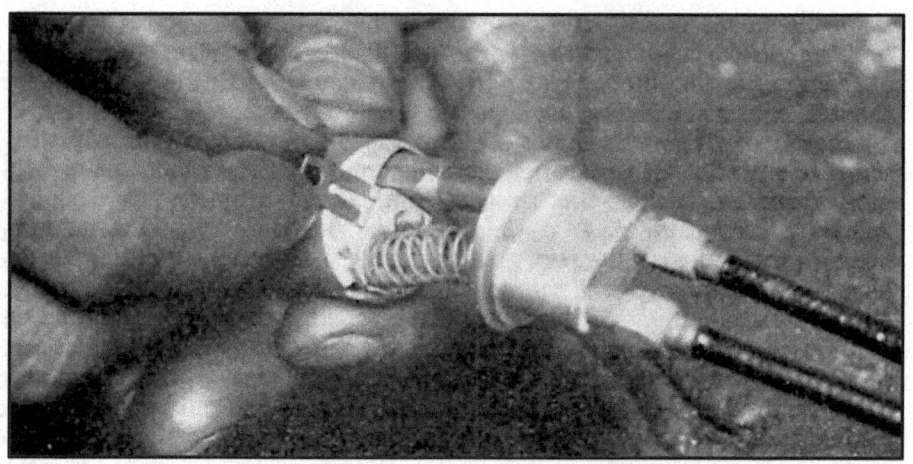

Fig. 10.—Setting the Position of the Tapered Jet Needle on the Amal Carburetter.
Note the clip that secures the needle by fitting into one of the grooves.

Type 6 valve and had a cut away of $\frac{4}{16}$, i.e. $\frac{1}{4}$ inch. In the majority of cases a No. 5 valve is standard for single-cylinder engines whilst for multi-cylinder engines a No. 4 is invariably the best.

Setting Position of Taper Needle

The routine for testing is as follows. With the air lever opened to its fullest extent, open the throttle halfway and note the sound of the exhaust. It should have a crisp, lively beat. Next close the air valve slowly until it is slightly below the edge of throttle. If the exhaust note and engine speed remain practically unaltered, the needle position is correct.

If the characteristic signs of weakness are present, the taper needle must be raised a notch at a time until the engine performance is good. Check mixture by closing air valve slightly below throttle valve. If engine speeds up the mixture is too weak.

If the engine labours, throws out black smoke from the exhaust, and does not pick up readily when the throttle is opened, the taper needle must be lowered. Normally the needle should be in the third groove (counted from the blunt end), and provided the foregoing adjustments have been methodically made, the engine should have good power and acceleration combined with excellent petrol consumption.

Tuning for Extreme Economy in Fuel.—If fuel consumption is of greater importance than the highest possible performance, the needle may be lowered one notch after finding the best all-round setting.

TYPES OF MOTOR-CYCLE CARBURETTERS

Tuning for Maximum Power.—If speed and power are of primary importance the main jet should be increased in size over that found by the above routine and the air lever may be left wide open.

Normal Fuel Consumption

It is a common belief that fuel consumption depends only on carburetter adjustment, but there are many other factors which seriously influence it, such as, general condition of engine, bad driving, excessive hill-climbing, incorrect gear ratio, sidecar out of line, and average driving

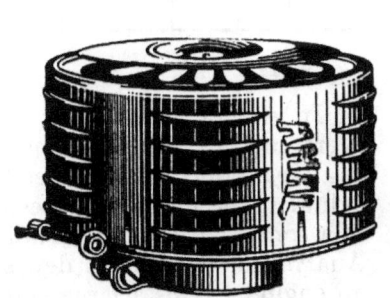
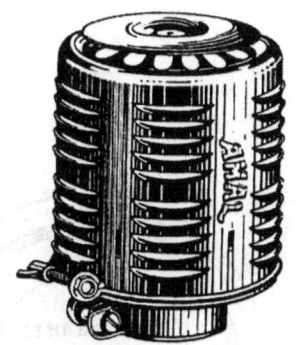
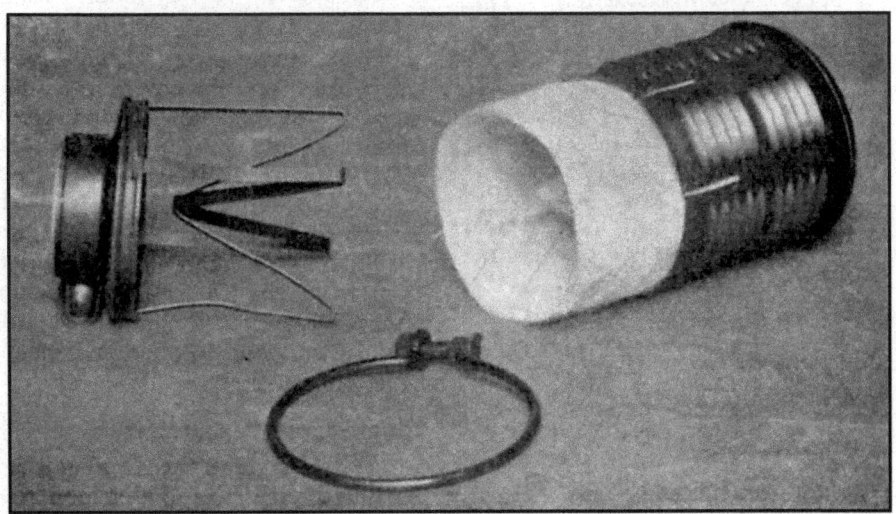

Fig. 11.—(*Above*) THE SHORT AND LONG MODELS OF THE AMAL AIR CLEANER. (*Below*) A CLEANER DISMANTLED.

TYPES OF MOTOR-CYCLE CARBURETTERS

speed. The following table gives the fuel consumption figures that can be reasonably expected under ordinary conditions while averaging 30 miles per hour:

Engine Capacity	Solo		Sidecar	
	Gear Ratio	M.p.g.	Gear Ratio	M.p.g.
250 c.c.	6/1	95–100	—	—
350 c.c.	5·5/1	85–90	6/1	70
500 c.c.	5/1	80–85	5·5/1	65–70
600 c.c.	4·7/1	70–80	5·5/1	60–65
750 c.c. Twin	—	—	5·5/1	55–60
1,000 c.c. Twin	4/1	55–60	5/1	50–55

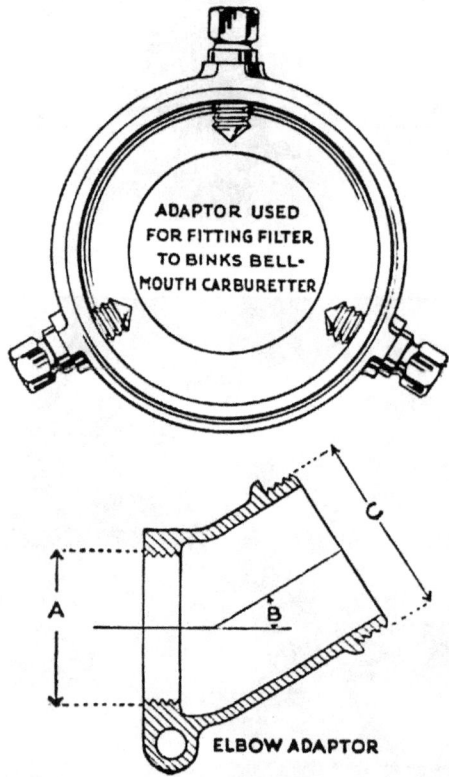

Fig. 12.—Elbow Adapters can be obtained for fitting Air Cleaners in those instances where they cannot be fitted directly on the Carburetter.

Air Filters

In view of the fact that almost every motor-cycle relies upon air as a means of cooling the head and cylinder, the engine is necessarily in a somewhat exposed condition. Analysis of the carbon deposit in an engine reveals a large percentage of road grit of a nature very destructive to cylinder walls, pistons, rings, etc., and the fitting of an *efficient* air filter is an excellent investment. The Amal air filter can be supplied to fit any make of motor-cycle carburetter, and in those instances where it cannot be screwed directly to the carburetter, a variety of adapters and elbows are available.

It is often possible to reduce somewhat the jet size after fitting an air cleaner, and the usual tests should be made to check whether this is necessary.

Single-lever Carburetter

Where desired the Amal can be supplied with a handlebar control for the throttle only. For starting purposes the air slide is moved by

TYPES OF MOTOR-CYCLE CARBURETTERS

means of a rod control fixed in the top of the mixing chamber, there being only two positions, " closed " for starting and " open " for general running. The same methods of tuning as for two-lever carburetters are employed.

The Amal Track-racing Carburetter

Although this model will give excellent results with ordinary petrol or benzole mixture, it has been designed mainly for use with alcohol and the various special fuels used for track racing. Whilst it has a pilot, a bypass and an air-adjusting screw for slow running and ease of starting, the ordinary air valve in the form of a slide is not used. For racing purposes where power alone counts, it is essential that the freest possible passage should be given to the air passing through the carburetter into the cylinder head, and the Amal track-racing carburetter has an absolutely clear throughway. The mixture is controlled by an air valve situated on the outside of the carburetter body, which, while performing the same duty as the air slide in the ordinary type of carburetter, does not cause any obstruction. The approximate choke and jet size for petrol and the best-known alcohol fuels are given below.

Fig. 13.—THE AMAL RACING-TYPE CARBURETTER, WITH TWIN FLOAT CHAMBERS FOR ALCOHOL FUELS.

APPROX. CHOKES AND SETTINGS—FOUR-STROKE O.H.V.

Engine capacity	Carb. type No.	Type No. denoting bore size	Bore inches	Valve	Jet size in c.c. for		
					Petrol	P.M.S.2 R.D.2	R.D.1
175 { 150	26	36	·81	12	140	220	260
{	26	42	·875	12	160	260	300
250	26	48	·937	12	200	325	350
350 {	26	55	1·0	12	240	400	450
{	27	62	1·06	12	280	450	500
500 {	27	67	1·12	12	325	500	600
{	27	75	1·18	12	350	550	650
600	27	83	1·25	12	400	650	700

In the case of multi-cylinder engines, take capacity of one cylinder.

TYPES OF MOTOR-CYCLE CARBURETTERS

Tuning Instruction for the Amal Track-racing Carburetter

The methods for tuning this carburetter are very similar in principle to those employed in their ordinary types, the chief exception being that there is no tapered jet needle. It will be noticed that with alcohol fuel the jet sizes are very much larger than when using petrol, and petrol pipes of at least ¼-inch bore should be used, and for engines of more than 350-c.c. capacity, twin float chambers are recommended in order that there should be no possible shortage of fuel supply to the engine. Care must also be taken that the petrol pipe does not run in a horizontal direction for any distance, or air locks may form and cause an erratic fuel feed to the carburetter.

The first step in tuning up is to check up the size of the main jet. A size should be chosen which gives maximum power and speed with the throttle wide open and also full air, which in this model enters from the side of the carburetter body through a small upright slot, the size of which is controlled by the air lever. By closing this slot the mixture strength can be made 50 per cent. richer and the air lever should again be used as a check on the main jet size. Should the power fall off when the air opening is closed halfway, it is a sure indication that the main jet is too large, whilst an increase in power shows that a larger jet should be used.

The next step is to tune the idling or slow-running device. This is similar in construction to that used in the standard Amal carburetter, the method of adjusting which has already been described and therefore need not be repeated. The approximate needle opening for petrol is two and a half turns, but for alcohol, less air is needed and the adjustment will probably have to be reduced to half a turn. As the adjustment of the idling needle affects the mixture " coming off " the idling, it should preferably be left a little on the rich side, as this will obviate any tendency for a weak spot when the bypass hole is feeding fuel and also help acceleration.

Intermediate Speeds

In the track-racing model, the throttle cut away affects the performance over a much larger range than in the standard carburetter, and its influence must be checked between one-eighth and three-quarter throttle opening. As before, the amount of cut away is stamped on top of the throttle valve in sixteenths of an inch, e.g. No. 9 having $\frac{9}{16}$ inch cut away, and a No. 12 $\frac{12}{16}$ inch or $\frac{3}{4}$ inch cut away, the latter being the standard supplied for all engines. It is possible, however, that due to some peculiarity in the engine another size may give better results, spitting back through the carburetter indicating too weak a mixture, calling therefore for a throttle valve with less cut away. Conversely, if the engine labours, thumps or shows signs of an excess of fuel, a larger cut away should be used. On no account should any attempt be made to adjust the mixture strength at full throttle by altering the cut away, as

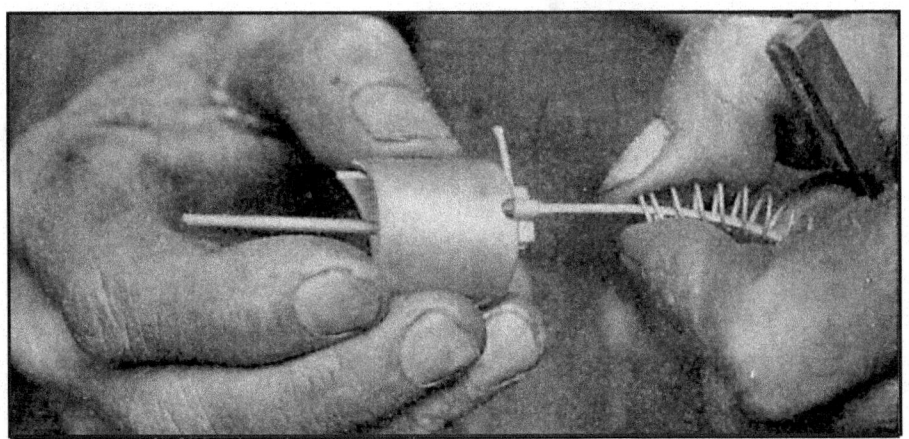

Fig. 14.—Disconnecting the Throttle Cable in the Amal Carburetter.
The split pin is pulled out, allowing the cable nipple to be withdrawn.

the latter ceases to have any influence after three-quarter throttle opening, the main jet being the sole deciding factor for full throttle. Changes in fuel do not affect the amount of cut away, which can remain the same whether pure petrol or alcohol, or alcohol mixtures are used.

Cleaning the Amal Carburetter

If the following routine is adopted and ordinary care and suitable tools used, the carburetter can be stripped without fear of damaging it or altering its adjustment. Reference should be made to Fig. 7 on page 8, and it will probably be found easier to slacken off bolt Q and union E if the carburetter is left bolted to the engine. Once these two are loosened the carburetter can be removed from the induction pipe stump and the remainder of the stripping proceeded with as follows :

(1) Unscrew the petrol-pipe unions and remove petrol pipe.

(2) Remove carburetter from engine by unscrewing the clip pin or flange nuts.

(3) Completely remove bolt Q and float chamber, the two fibre washers being placed on the bolt to avoid losing them.

(4) Unscrew the lock ring on top of mixing chamber and carefully withdraw the throttle valve, and in the case of the standard carburetter the air valve also, special care being taken in the latter model to avoid damaging the taper needle. Remove needle by gently levering out to one side the copper-coloured clip, first noting in which needle groove it is fixed.

(5) Completely unscrew union nut E from bottom of mixing chamber (there is a fibre washer in the recess at the top of the nut) and push out the jet block F. If this is tight, a piece of wood should be placed in the top

TYPES OF MOTOR-CYCLE CARBURETTERS

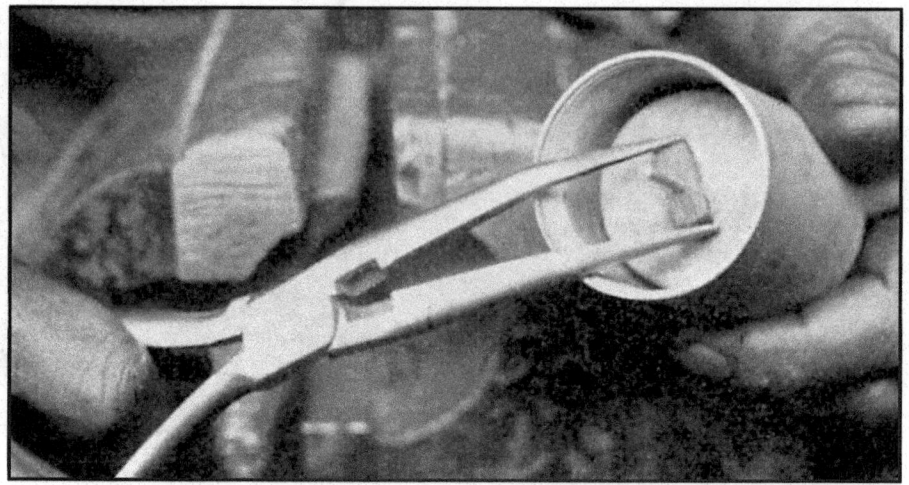

Fig. 15.—Removing the Float Needle in the Amal Carburetter.
The ends of the clip are slightly squeezed together to clear the groove in the float needle. The latter will then drop out from the bottom of the float chamber.

of the carburetter and gently tapped till the jet block is loosened. Unscrew main jet P and needle jet O.

(6) Slacken off lock screw X and unscrew the float-chamber cover.

(7) Pinch clip V inwards with the thumb and forefinger and lift it off the float needle. As this will release the needle, care must be taken to prevent it dropping where it might roll away and be lost, or damaged through falling on a hard surface.

(8) Wash all parts in clean petrol and check the following :

(9) Point of float chamber needle. If a distinct ridge is seen, replace with new needle as soon as possible.

(10) Test throttle valve for sloppiness in mixing chamber. If much play is present, a new valve should be fitted.

(11) Clip holding throttle needle. It is essential that this holds the needle firmly. If the needle turns freely, the groove will be rapidly worn, thus allowing the needle to move up and down and thereby causing varying mixture strength.

(12) See that the pilot jet J and the pilot outlet M in the mixing chamber are clear, as any obstruction here will cause bad idling and starting. A fine bristle is the best means for cleaning these passages.

Reassembling the Carburetter

(1) Fit the jet block to the mixing chamber, taking note that the locating pin on side fits into the slot cut for its reception. Screw on lightly the mixing-chamber union nut complete with its fibre washer.

TYPES OF MOTOR-CYCLE CARBURETTERS

(2) Screw in the main jet, and in the case of the standard carburetter the needle jet which carries it.

(3) Open throttle lever halfway (in standard model, air lever to be opened ⅞ inch) and insert the whole assembly carefully into the mixing chamber, with the cut away towards the air intake, twisting it to and fro until the air valve is felt to enter the slot cut for it in the jet block. Care must also be taken to see that the tapered needle enters the hole in the centre of the jet block. Further careful manipulation will enable the throttle valve to slide into position, there being also a ridge on one side of the jet block to locate the throttle accurately. Having successfully manœuvred the throttle and air valve into place, the mixing chamber lock nut can be screwed into position, due attention being given to the slot in the mixing chamber itself, which takes the small projection at the mixing chamber top to prevent it moving from its correct position when the locking ring is tightened up.

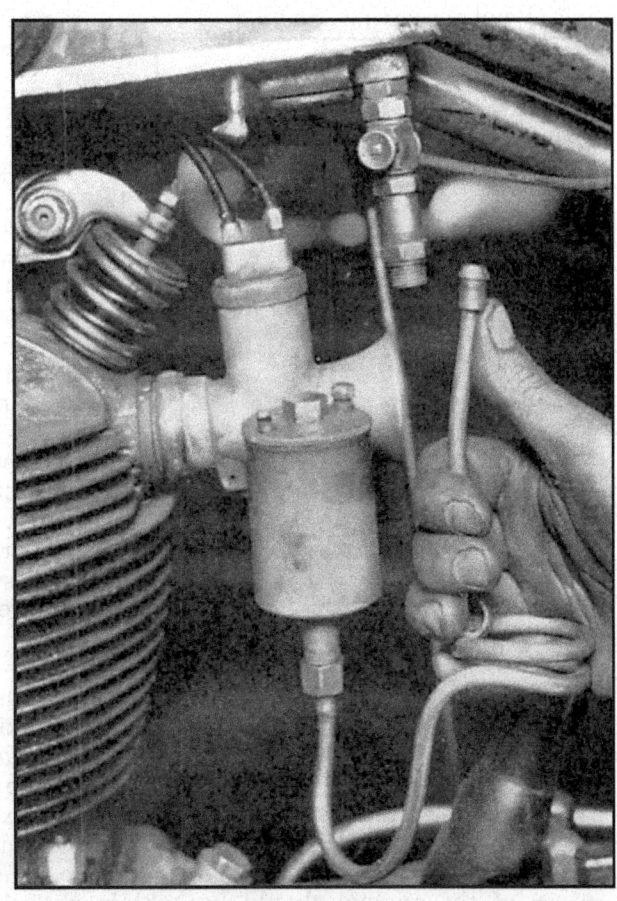

Fig. 16.—Set the Petrol Feed Pipe so that the Nipple easily registers with the Union.

Avoid having to strain the pipe and union nut to fit the threads, or petrol pipes will fracture and soldered tank connections break away.

(4) Fix the carburetter to the engine, making sure that in the case of the slip-type fitting the carburetter is pushed right home on the induction pipe stump, and in the case of a flange fitting

TYPES OF MOTOR-CYCLE CARBURETTERS

that the gasket is not broken or too hard through prolonged use or heat.

(5) Tighten up the union nut E.

(6) Offer up the float chamber, and tighten in position by means of the bolt Q, not forgetting the all-important fibre washers, one on each side of the lug through which the bolt Q passes.

(7) The float, float needle and clip may now be assembled, and it will be necessary to hold the lower end of the needle up on to its seating by means of a pencil point or similar-shaped article, whilst the clip is slid into its correct place, the groove in the needle. The curved part of the clip is next to the float. Screw on the float-chamber cover and lock in position by tightening screw X.

(8) Blow out the petrol pipe, clean the filter if one is fitted, and reassemble.

(9) Warm up engine and check the pilot setting in case this has been altered during the cleaning process.

NOTE.—If it is desired to assemble completely the carburetter without fixing same to the engine, on no account should it be held in a vice while the float-chamber fixing bolt or mixing-chamber union nut are tightened. A piece of hardwood, or better still, a piece of brass rod the same size as the induction stump of the engine, should be held in the vice and the carburetter body pushed on to it. If the body is bruised or squeezed out of shape, the throttle and air slide will bind, and any attempt to file or ease these parts will only cause air leaks and faulty running.

Fig. 17.—THE 1930-1 TWO-LEVER MODEL BINKS CARBURETTER.

THE 1930-1 BINKS CARBURETTER (TYPES 47, 48 AND 49)

Manufacturers: AMALGAMATED CARBURETTERS, LTD., Holford Works, Perry Barr, Birmingham. Telephone: Birmingham East 1371-2-3-4-5. Telegrams: Amalcarb, Phone, Birmingham.

With the exception of certain improvements in construction, these carburetters retain the basic principles which have characterised them for

TYPES OF MOTOR-CYCLE CARBURETTERS

the past few years. The two-jet system is still used, with the exception of the special model for the Scott motor-cycle, which has three jets. A throttle stop has been incorporated on all models except type " LR " to enable " idling " to be adjusted to a nicety with the throttle lever in the closed position.

Single- or double-lever control can be incorporated, the former being mainly used for stationary engine work.

Construction

A section through the carburetter is shown in Fig. 18, A being the carburetter body or mixing chamber. The jet block B is held on to the lower side of the body by means of the union nut E, a fibre washer F being necessary to ensure a petrol-tight joint.

The layout of the float-chamber mechanism is very similar to the Amal carburetter, with the exception that a gauze filter is inserted in a recess immediately below the float-chamber needle. The pilot jet is shown at C, whilst D indicates the main jet, the longer of the two.

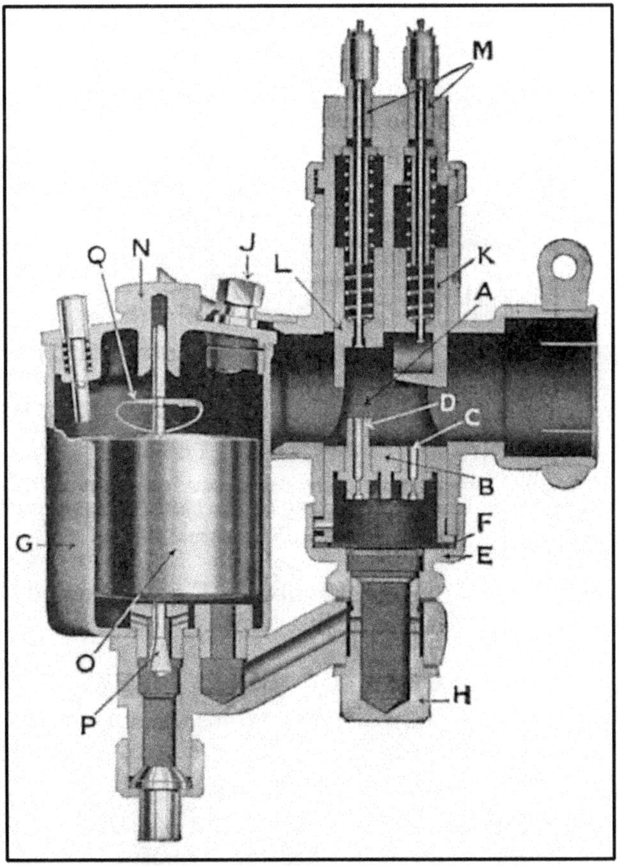

In the extension above the mixing chamber are located the throttle valve K and the air valve L, whilst in the small diagram is shown the throttle stop screw which sets the throttle valve for idling, it being prevented from moving by means of a lock nut.

Assuming the float chamber to be filled with fuel, the throttle valve slightly open and the engine revolved, the rush of air through the passage A will draw fuel from the pilot jet C, which, owing to the fact that it is

Fig. 18.—A SECTION THROUGH THE 1930–1 BINKS CARBURETTER, SHOWING GENERAL LAYOUT OF PARTS.

TYPES OF MOTOR-CYCLE CARBURETTERS

immediately under the throttle valve, is subjected to a high degree of suction. With the throttle in the idling position, no fuel issues from the main jet D, the air speed past it being too low to affect it. As the throttle is opened the suction on the pilot jet decreases, but begins to affect the main jet, and provided the jets are correctly chosen, the take over from pilot to main jet will be perfectly smooth.

TUNING INSTRUCTIONS

The following routine should be adopted if the Binks carburetter is to be successfully tuned.

(1) Select the correct size of main jet from the table on page 23. This affects the performance from five-eighths to full throttle opening.

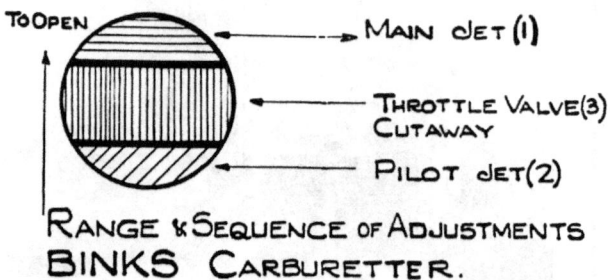

Fig. 19.—THE RANGE AND SEQUENCE OF ADJUSTMENTS RELATIVE TO THROTTLE OPENING OF THE BINKS CARBURETTER. Compare this with the Amal, Fig. 9.

(2) Choose next the pilot jet, which must be of such a size that from the closed or idling position to quarter open throttle the mixture is correct.

(3) Finally decide the amount of throttle cut away that gives good results with the throttle valve between one-quarter and five-eighths open. Fig. 19 shows diagrammatically the order and range of these adjustments.

SELECTION OF BINKS CARBURETTER AND JETS

The table on page 23 enables the correct size and type of carburetter to be chosen, together with the size of main and pilot jets as close as it is possible to give them.

Main Jet

This should be checked for correctness of size with the air lever three-quarters open if the motor-cycle is to be used for ordinary work. If the engine speeds up when the throttle is opened more than this amount the jet is too large. On the other hand, too small a jet will be indicated by an increase in speed when the throttle is slightly closed below the three-quarter open position.

Pilot Jet

As this affects mainly the idling, but also, to a certain extent, the take over on to the main jet, a compromise must be struck between the

TYPES OF MOTOR-CYCLE CARBURETTERS

STANDARD SETTINGS FOR FOUR-STROKE SINGLE-CYLINDER ENGINES

For Petrol, Benzole Mixture, Ethyl Petrol and Benzole

Engine	Carb. type No.	Bore size No.	Pilot jet	Main jet	Valve
50–75 c.c.	46	2B	20	—	2/2
75 to 100 c.c. {	46	3B	20	20	3/2
	46	7B	20	25	7/2
100 to 125 c.c.	46	10B	25	30	10/2
150 to 175 c.c.	46	14B	25	40	14/2
175 c.c.—					
S.V. Touring	46	14B	25	40	14/2
O.H.V. Touring	47	17B	30	50	47/2
O.H.V. Sports	47	21B	30	60	47/2
O.H.V. Racing	47	25B	30	80	47/2
250 c.c.—					
S.V. Touring	47	21B	30	60	47/2
O.H.V. Touring	47	25B	30	70	47/2
O.H.V. Sports	47	25B	30	70	47/2
O.H.V. Racing	48	28B	35	90	48/2
O.H.V. Racing	48	33B	35	100	48/2
300 c.c.—					
S.V. Touring	47	21B	30	60	47/2
350 c.c.—					
S.V. Touring	47	25B	30	70	47/2
O.H.V. Touring	47	25B	30	70	47/2
O.H.V. Touring	48	28B	35	80	48/2
O.H.V. Sports	48	33B	35	90	48/2
O.H.V. Sports	49	39B	40	110	49/2
O.H.V. Racing	49	45B	40	130	49/2
500 c.c.—					
S.V. Touring	48	33B	35	100	48/2
S.V. Touring	49	39B	40	110	49/2
O.H.V. Touring	49	45B	40	130	49/2
O.H.V. Sports	49	45B	40	130	49/2
O.H.V. Sports	49	51B	40	140	49/2
O.H.V. Racing	49	51B	40	150	49/2
O.H.V. Racing	LR	1 3/32 inches	40	160	—
600 c.c.—					
S.V. Touring	49	39B	40	110	49/2
S.V. Touring	49	45B	40	130	49/2
O.H.V. Touring	49	45B	40	130	49/2
O.H.V. Sports	49	51B	40	140	49/2
O.H.V. Racing	LR	1 1/8 inches	40	190	—
O.H.V. Racing	—	—	—	—	—

two. If there is any tendency for a weak flat spot during the change over, a pilot jet one size larger will be necessary to eliminate it.

Throttle Valve Cut Away

Throttle valves with varying degrees of cut away are supplied and, as previously mentioned, the amount of cut away decides the mixture strength between three-eighths and five-eighths throttle opening. The amount is marked on the throttle, and varies from No. 0, which is flat, to No. 5, which has five-sixteenths cut away.

TYPES OF MOTOR-CYCLE CARBURETTERS

Fig. 20.—Removing Jets from Binks Carburetter by Special Key.
Note the recess into which the jets are fitted, necessitating the use of the special key.

Starting a Cold Engine

Slightly flood the carburetter by means of the tickler, open throttle about one-eighth, set ignition lever three-quarters of the way to full advance, and start engine in the usual manner. When engine is properly warmed up adjust the throttle-stop screw to give the desired degree of idling or tickover.

General Maintenance and Cleaning

As a filter is fitted, it is unlikely that any trouble will be experienced with jet stoppage. The usual care in handling the parts should of course be observed, and the carburetter can with advantage be periodically stripped for cleaning and the parts washed in clean petrol. By unscrewing the jet plug H, the float chamber can be removed, the method employed in taking this to pieces being the same as for the Amal carburetter.

The jet block can be withdrawn when the union nut E is unscrewed, and the jets unscrewed from it by means of the special key supplied with each carburetter. The jet block is prevented from turning from its correct position by a small pin which fits in a slot in the mixing chamber, and the mixing-chamber top is also located in a similar fashion.

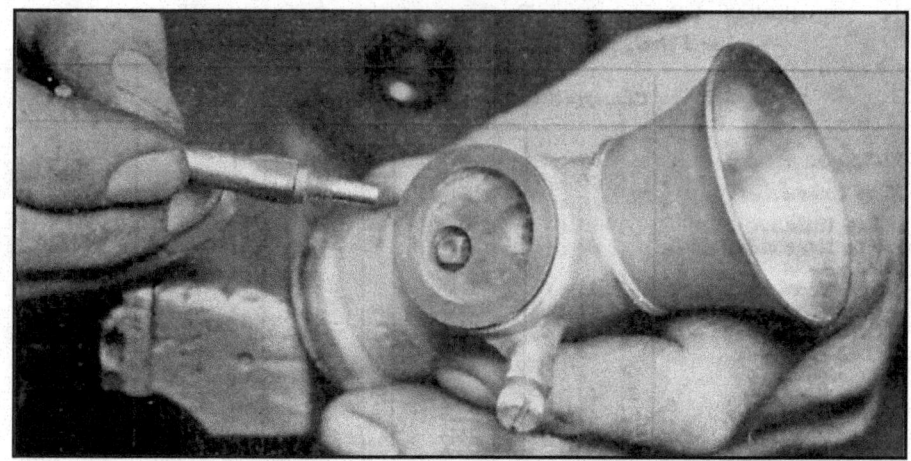

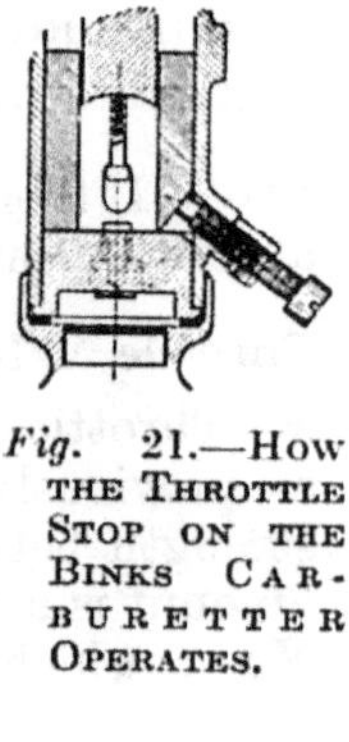

Fig. 21.—How the Throttle Stop on the Binks Carburetter Operates.

Use of Alcohol Fuel in Binks Carburetter

The table of jet sizes on page 25 has been fixed for petrol, petrol-benzole mixtures, ethyl petrol and benzole,

TYPES OF MOTOR-CYCLE CARBURETTERS

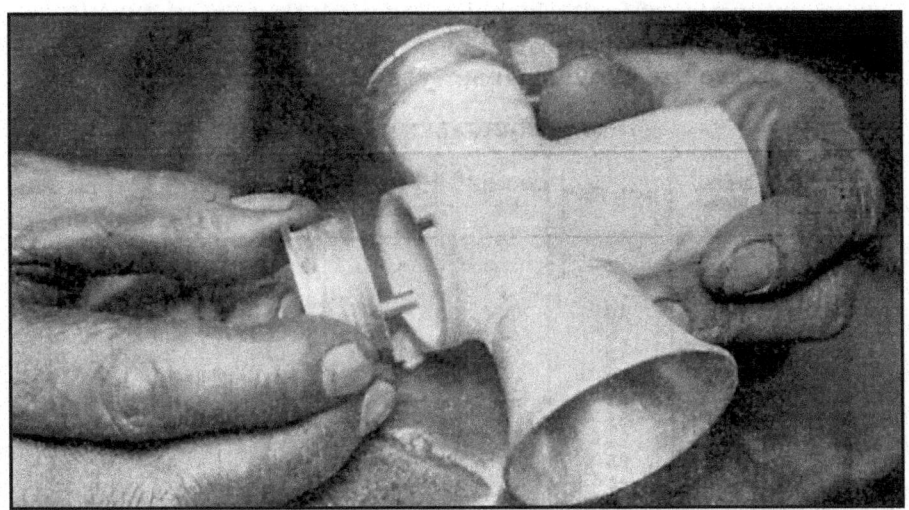

Fig. 22.—Binks Mixing Chamber, showing Pin in Jet Block and the Slot into which this Fits.

and the following increase in the flow of both main and pilot jets must be given if alcohol fuels are used in Binks carburetters.

Jet size for Petrol and Petrol-Benzole, c.c.	Jet size for P.M.S.2 and R.D.2	Jet size for R.D.1	Jet size for Petrol and Petrol-Benzole, c.c.	Jet size for P.M.S.2 and R.D.2	Jet size for R.D.1
25	40	45	140	220	260
30	45	55	160	260	300
35	55	65	180	280	325
40	60	75	200	300	375
50	80	90	220	350	400
60	95	110	240	375	450
70	110	130	260	400	475
80	120	150	280	450	525
90	140	170	300	475	550
100	160	180	325	500	600
120	180	220	350	550	650

Interchangeability of Parts in New and Old Type Binks Carburetters

In all cases the reference number on the side of the mixing chamber should be quoted when ordering spare parts, as some 1929 parts cannot be used in 1930 models, and vice versa.

Jet Markings for Amal and Binks Carburetters

Originally, jets were known by the diameter of the hole through them, but the method now employed is to mark them with the amount (in

TYPES OF MOTOR-CYCLE CARBURETTERS

cubic centimetres of fuel) which flows through them in a given time and under strictly standardised conditions. The following table is given so that the relative size of old and new type jets can be compared:

JET EQUIVALENTS LIST

Amal, B. & B. Amal, Binks. Flow in c.c.	Jet dia. inch.	Amac No.	Old Binks No.	Amal, B. & B. Amal, Binks. Flow in c.c.	Jet dia. inch.	Amac No.	Old Binks No.
15	—	—	0	100	·034	32	11
20	·015	—	1	110	·035	33	13
25	—	16	2	120	·037	35	14
30	·018	18	3	130	·038	36	15
35	—	19	4	140	·040	38	16
40	·021	20	—	150	·041	39	17
45	—	21	—	160	·043	40	18
50	·024	23	5	170	·044	41	19
55	—	24	—	180	·045	43	20
60	·026	25	6	200	·048	45	21
65	—	26	—	220	·050	47	22
70	·028	27	7	240	·052	49	23
75	—	28	—	260	·055	51	24
80	·030	29	8	280	·057	53	25
85	—	—	—	300	·059	55	26
90	·032	30	9	325	—	57	—
95	—	31	—	350	—	59	—

NOTE.—1929 and 1930 Amal and Binks jets are not interchangeable with those of other years' manufacture.

Binks Special Three-jet Carburetter for Scott Motor-cycles, 1929-30-1 Models

This carburetter has been specially designed for the Scott motor-cycle, a twin-cylinder water-cooled machine of the highest merit. Although this carburetter has three jets, it must not be confused with the early model Binks three-jet damping carburetter. This new model is an elaboration of the latest type two-jet Binks carburetter, and owing to the fact that the induction flange on the Scott engine is on the slope, the construction is such that, whilst the float chamber is of necessity upright, the body or mixing chamber slopes downwards to meet the engine induction port.

The jets are arranged in the following order, taken from the engine end: the pilot jet, the power jet and the main jet. Idling is controlled solely by the pilot jet, and the smallest jet should be chosen that will enable the engine to tick over when warmed up. Up to half throttle opening the mixture is fixed by the pilot and main jets, and a main jet should be used that gives good pickup and regular two-stroking from idling to half throttle. From there on, to full throttle opening, the power jet comes into use, so that all three jets supply fuel at full throttle. In selecting the power jet, care must be taken that when considering the

TYPES OF MOTOR-CYCLE CARBURETTERS

Fig. 23.—THE FILTER UNDER THE JET BLOCK OF THE BINKS CARBURETTER.

question of consumption, this is not overdone, as too small a power jet will cause overheating of the engine and plug trouble.

Cleaning and Assembling

The same routine should be adopted as for the standard two-jet Binks model, as the constructional details are almost identical. The jets are of the short pattern, the tubes being permanently fixed in the mixing chamber.

The standard setting for the Flying Squirrel Scott is main jet 110, power jet 50, pilot jet 30. As air leaks will affect the carburation and make tuning difficult and unreliable, particular care should be taken to see that the flange gasket and flange faces are in good order, and that the flange is not bent through carelessness in tightening the fixing bolts. These should be tightened alternately a little at a time until both are quite tight. If one bolt is pulled up deadtight before the other, the carburetter flange is almost certain to be distorted.

THE VILLIERS MOTOR-CYCLE CARBURETTER

Manufacturers: THE VILLIERS ENGINEERING CO., LTD., Marston Road, Wolverhampton, England. Telephone: Wolverhampton, 1666-7-8. Telegrams: " Villiers, Wolverhampton."

Two models are made, the single-lever and the double-lever types. Both are almost identical in construction, the single-lever model having a taper jet needle which has to be adjusted in position from the top of the carburetter itself, whilst in the double-lever model the needle position can be controlled by means of a lever on the handlebars of the machine.

TYPES OF MOTOR-CYCLE CARBURETTERS

SINGLE-LEVER MODEL

This consists of a horizontal mixing chamber on the top of which is a piston-type throttle valve. The float-chamber mechanism is situated directly under the mixing chamber, and can be removed by unscrewing one nut. The jet system is a simple one, the jet opening being controlled relative to the throttle opening by means of a taper needle mounted in the throttle in such a way that as the throttle is opened, the needle is partly withdrawn from the jet, thereby allowing more fuel to pass.

The position of the needle relative to the throttle can be varied by screwing it up or down in the throttle valve itself.

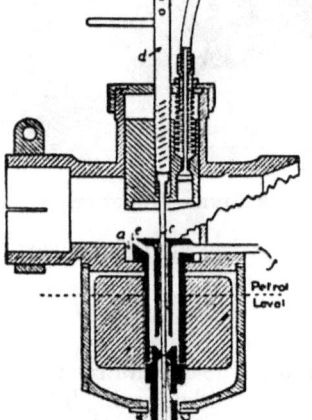

Fig. 24.—SECTION OF VILLIERS SINGLE-LEVER CARBURETTER.

Tuning

This consists of finding two things, the correct taper for the needle and its position in the throttle valve relative to the jet. To start the engine, turn the needle adjusting rod (a small lever standing out to one side on top of the carburetter) as far as it will go to the left, open throttle about a quarter of its full movement, press tickler for a second or two until fuel appears, and start up the engine. Allow the engine to run until it reaches normal working temperature, and then slowly close throttle to slow-running speed. Next turn needle bar to the right (clockwise when viewed from above) until correct mixture for slow running is obtained, and then open up the throttle quickly. The engine should accelerate smoothly and develop full power if the taper of the needle is correct. If, however, the engine misses and spitting back takes place in the carburetter, it is a sign that the needle is not suitable, and another should be fitted that has a bigger taper, so that at full throttle a bigger area of jet is given. On the other hand, if the engine hunts and throws black smoke out of the exhaust through overrichness, a needle should be used with less taper. When the correct needle has been found, the mixture strength should be correct at all engine speeds and throttle openings.

If when turning the needle bar it is found that insufficient movement can be given to it, the bar or lever should be unscrewed and the needle itself screwed up or down until the correct slow-running position has been found. The bar can then be screwed back into a convenient hole. It is essential, however, that the bar be so set that in the full weak position the needle setting gives a mixture just too weak to run on, so that the bar must be moved some little way towards the rich position to get a satisfactory performance.

TYPES OF MOTOR-CYCLE CARBURETTERS

The Taper Needle

The degree of taper of the needle is indicated by a number stamped on the side, these being as follows : 2, $2\frac{1}{2}$, 3, $3\frac{1}{2}$, 4, $4\frac{1}{2}$, 5, 6, 7 and 8.

Jets

Centre pieces with different sizes of jet can be supplied. These are marked on the side, and are numbered 1, 3, 5 or 6. A normal two-stroke engine requires a smaller jet than a four-stroke engine if steady two-stroking at low speeds is to be obtained, whilst in a four-stroke engine a larger jet will be required if a good tickover is desired when running out of gear. Correction of the mixture ratio is controlled basically by means of a compensating air tube, and on no account should this opening be blocked up by a screw or dirt or the performance of the carburetter will be completely spoilt.

Changing the Needle

First remove the throttle by unscrewing the cap on top, unscrew the bar from the needle rod, then the needle rod itself—taking care not to bend the needle—when the needle and the small spring under its head can be pushed out of the throttle. Slip the spring on the new needle, taking note that the small coil is at the top of the needle, replace in throttle, screw in needle bar and reassemble throttle needle-bar rod. To prevent any risk of loss the rod should be tightened into place with a pair of pliers when its correct hole has been found.

Cleaning

The carburetter should always be removed from the engine before dismantling the parts for cleaning, etc. Remove the throttle valve complete with needle, turn carburetter over so that the float chamber is on top, and on unscrewing the nut in its centre the float-chamber bowl can be lifted off. Care must be taken not to lose the fibre washer under the nut. The float and float-needle valve can then be taken off, also the large fibre washer on which the rim of the float-chamber bowl seats. The compensating tube should then be unscrewed, when the centre piece complete with jet will fall out through the bore in which the throttle slides. The centre piece has a fibre washer under its head and the jet should on no account be unscrewed from it.

After cleaning every part in petrol, reassemble as follows :

Put the correct fibre washer under the head of the centre piece and after placing in position screw compensating tube gently in. Next assemble the large fibre washer, the fuel needle and the float, taking care that the fuel needle is not inserted upside down in the seating. Following this comes the float-chamber bowl, a fibre washer and then the nut, the tightening of which holds everything firmly in position.

TYPES OF MOTOR-CYCLE CARBURETTERS

Needle Rod

Later models have a damper spring to prevent the needle from moving unless turned by hand, but earlier models relied on the outward spring of the slotted end of the needle. Should this type of needle become slack in the thread, the ends should be sprung apart by forcing in a piece of $\frac{3}{32}$-inch diameter rod, and closing the ends by means of a pair of pliers to form a bulge.

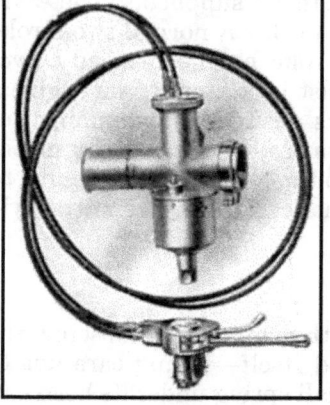

Fig. 25.—Villiers Two-lever Carburetter.

THE VILLIERS TWO-LEVER CARBURETTER

The method of tuning this model is identical with that used with the single-lever type, the handlebar control for the needle somewhat simplifying the operation. Having found a needle, the taper of which gives correct mixture strength under all conditions, the position of the needle in the throttle should be adjusted so that with the lever in the full-weak position, the mixture is just too weak. The actual position can be found by trial and error, the adjusting screw on the body of the control being screwed up or down until the correct height is found, when the lock nut should be tightened. Turning the screw inwards makes the mixture weaker and unscrewing makes it richer.

Needles and Jets

These are numbered as for the single-lever model, and the method of changing a needle is the same as used with the single-lever type, except that in place of the needlebar will be found a hexagon extension of the throttle, which must be unscrewed before the needle and spring can be taken out. When reassembling see that the control wire passes through the top ring that holds the throttle in place before screwing in the hexagon throttle extension; then place throttle in its barrel, locate the top disk in its correct position by means of the pip on its side and finally screw on the top ring.

A SIMPLE THEORY OF IGNITION

THE ignition system of the modern single- and twin-cylindered motor-cycle possesses all the essentials of its bigger brother, fitted to the 4-, 6-, 8- or even 12-cylinder car or aero engine. It differs, chiefly, in regard to the distributing arrangements for the high-tension current to the sparking plugs.

To the average motor-cyclist, the ignition system consists firstly of a small and very compact machine called a magneto, and secondly, a sparking plug, the two being electrically connected by means of rubber-insulated high-tension cable.

The Voltage of the Spark

In order to produce this spark it is necessary that a voltage of some 4,000 to 7,000 volts be generated. It is the duty of the magneto to generate this very high voltage, whilst the sparking plug serves as the means of producing the spark inside the cylinder or the engine. The H.T. cables provide the insulated path for the current of the spark, the return path being through the engine frame and the magneto housing.

Eighty-three Sparks every Second!

The magneto on the modern motor-cycle may be required to produce sparks, with unfailing regularity, at a rate of 5,000 per minute or 83 per second. Not only must a regular succession of sparks be produced, but also each spark must necessarily be very accurately timed to occur when the piston reaches some definite point on the compression stroke. Further, the magneto must be capable of generating its maximum voltage when starting, or at the very low speed of about 100 r.p.m.

About Insulation

It is well known that electricity always takes the path of least resistance, and particularly is this so at high voltages. Consequently, it is very necessary that the high-tension circuit should be thoroughly well insulated, in order that the H.T. current shall be confined to its proper path. This applies equally to all parts of the ignition system, whether magneto, sparking plug or the H.T. cable. Not only must the insulation be good in itself, but also the insulating surfaces must be as free as possible from moisture, dust or carbon deposition. All these are likely

A SIMPLE THEORY OF IGNITION

to cause leakage of the H.T. current, and the best results are only obtained if all parts of the ignition system are maintained as clean and dry as possible.

Have you experienced this?

For instance, excessive moisture or dirt accumulation on the plug insulator may cause difficult starting, and in very humid atmosphere the spark may jump over the external surface of the plug insulator rather than across the plug gap in the cylinder. Similarly, excessive carbon deposition on the plug insulator inside the cylinder may result in poor starting or misfiring.

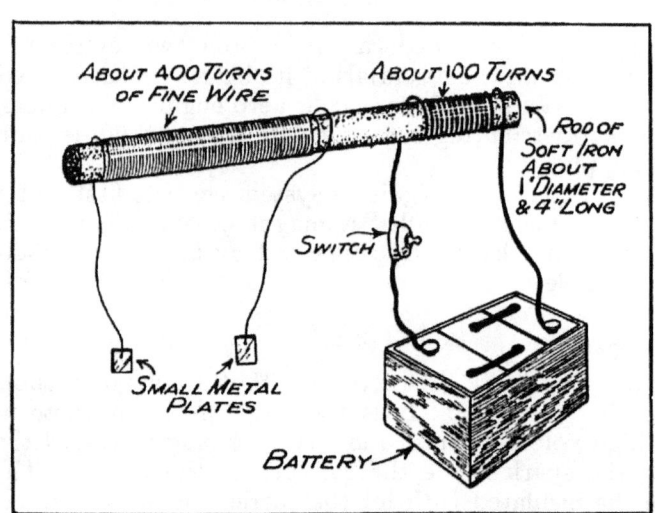

Fig. 1.—MAKE THE SIMPLE EXPERIMENT ILLUSTRATED ABOVE AND EXPLAINED IN THE TEXT, AND YOU WILL OBTAIN A PRACTICAL ILLUSTRATION OF THE WAY IN WHICH BOTH COILS AND MAGNETOS WORK.

A clear understanding of the simple fact that clean and dry insulations greatly minimise leakage of the H.T. current will enable motor-cyclists to detect and remedy one of the most common sources of ignition trouble.

THE PRINCIPLES OF ELECTRICAL IGNITION SIMPLY EXPLAINED

An Ordinary Electric Circuit

If we connect an electric lamp to the two terminals of a battery, the filament will immediately become incandescent. Now the battery is merely a source of electrical pressure or voltage, and when the lamp filament is connected to the battery terminals a current or flow of electricity is produced, and it is the heating effect of this current that causes incandescence of the filament. In this respect the battery is like an oil pump, which creates a pressure of oil, and thereby produces a flow of oil in the engine.

A SIMPLE THEORY OF IGNITION

About Magnets

Everyone is familiar with a permanent magnet, and knows that it has certain properties, such as the attraction of iron and the attraction or repulsion of another magnet. These properties are due to invisible and innumerable magnetic lines of force, which are associated with a permanent magnet and permeate the space surrounding the magnet.

If we wind a bar of soft iron with turns of insulated wire and pass an electric current through the wire, the soft iron will behave exactly like a permanent magnet *as long as the current is flowing through the wire wound on the iron bar*. Such a magnet is called an *electromagnet*.

An Instructive Experiment

The reader should make the simple experiment illustrated in Fig. 1. Having wound a soft-iron bar with two separate windings, and connected the thicker winding to a battery through a switch, hold with the hands the ends of the fine wire winding whilst the switch is rapidly closed and opened. It will be found that a slight shock will be experienced, thereby indicating that a voltage very much greater than that of the battery has been induced in the fine-wire or secondary winding, which is in no way electrically connected to the battery.

The Explanation

The explanation is really very simple. When the switch is closed, current flows in what we will call the primary winding. This current induces or creates magnetic lines in the iron bar and the surrounding space which become linked with the secondary winding. During the time these lines of force are being induced or built up an electrical pressure or voltage is induced in the secondary winding. On opening the switch the primary winding current is interrupted, resulting in the disappearance of the magnetic lines, and in consequence of their collapse a voltage is again induced in the secondary winding, but this time in the opposite direction to that when the switch was closed.

What the Experiment Shows

Thus, we see that, whenever magnetic lines of force are caused to become linked with a winding, or when present are dissociated from the winding, an electro-motive force or voltage is induced in that winding. *The voltage will only be induced as long as the number of magnetic lines linked with the winding is changing.*

The Ignition Coil

In the experiment described we have the main essentials of the coil-ignition system, viz. a battery, a soft-iron core wound with primary and

A SIMPLE THEORY OF IGNITION

secondary winding, and means for rapidly making and breaking the primary circuit. By the experiment we have illustrated the principle underlying the operation of the induction or spark coil.

The Magneto is a " Coil " Generating its own Primary Current

In the modern magneto a primary winding, consisting of some 200 turns of fairly thick enamel-covered wire, and a secondary winding of about 10,000 turns of extremely fine-gauge enamel-covered wire are wound on a soft-iron core, called an armature, which rotates between the poles of a permanent magnet.

Considering for a moment the primary winding only, the rotation of the armature results in changes in the magnetic lines or flux passing through the soft-iron core, and since the primary winding is wound on this core, a voltage will be induced in it. Every time this current is interrupted by the contact breaker, a high voltage is set up in the secondary winding.

Since the primary current is induced by rotating the armature in a magnetic field, the magneto is a self-contained unit, quite independent of a battery. Apart from this, its operation is very similar to the coil-ignition system. The contact breaker, which is carried at the end of the armature and serves to interrupt the primary current, is arranged to close when the induced primary voltage is zero, and to open in the fully advanced position when the primary current is a maximum. As there are two positions of the armature for each revolution at which the primary voltage and current are a maximum, this type of magneto is capable of giving two sparks per revolution of the armature spindle.

MOTOR-CYCLE IGNITION
FROM THE PRACTICAL SIDE
By Leon Griffiths, A.M.I.E.E., A.M.I.A.E.

Fig. 1.—Removing a Magneto Armature.

The amateur is warned against removing the armature of a magneto, as this may weaken the magneto. Figs. 19, 20 and 21 show how a skilled repairer tests an armature, and how the magnets are afterwards remagnetised.

AS the present work is essentially practical, we are dealing first with the practical side of this important subject. We believe that the motor-cyclist or garage man who wants to trace or remedy a fault in the ignition will prefer to obtain the practical information without having first to read through the theory, interesting and important though this is.

A later article will deal simply with the theory and construction of magnetos.

INSTALLATION AND MAINTENANCE

Motor-cycle magnetos are generally mounted on a platform, either machined on the crankcase or provided by a separate bracket, being secured in position by means of screws or clamps. The drive is usually by means of a roller chain from the crankshaft or by a gear engaging the timing gear.

MOTOR-CYCLE IGNITION

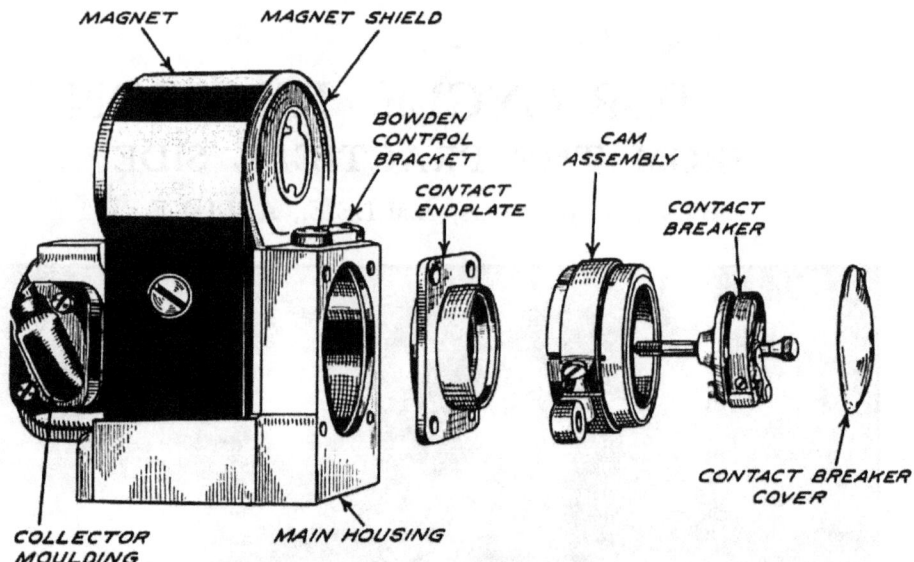

Fig. 2.—Exploded View of B.T.H. Type K2 Magneto.

To obviate a multiplicity of types for motor-cycles, and also to facilitate replacement, British manufacturers supply two main types of magneto ("K" and "M"), having dimensions in accordance with the standards fixed some years ago by the British Engineering Standards Association and given in B.E.S.A. Specification No. 5027—1924. The important differences of these two types are the height of the spindle centre from the base and the size of the tapered spindle end to which the sprocket or gear wheel is fitted. The "K" type base is machined to give a spindle height of 45 mm., and the "M" type 35 mm., the allowed

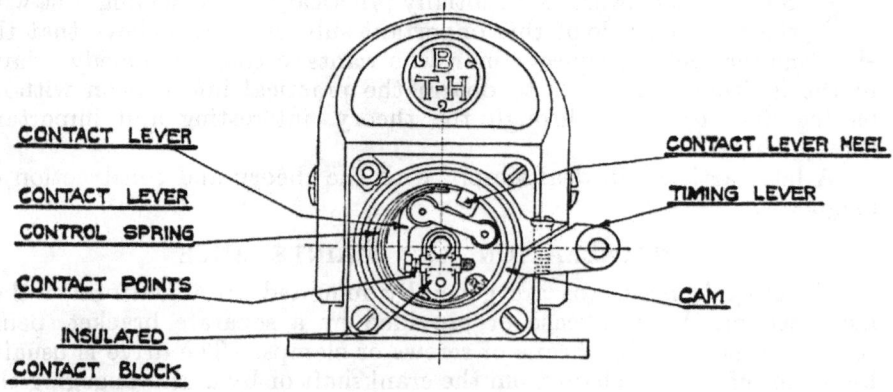

Fig. 3.—End View of B.T.H. Type M2 Magneto, showing Contact Breaker.

MOTOR-CYCLE IGNITION

tolerance being — ·003 inch. This fine machining tolerance is necessary to obviate undue variations in gear meshing, when gear drive is employed.

INSTALLATION

Mounting a Chain Drive Magneto

When fitting a magneto the first precaution is to see that no undue strain is imposed on the magneto spindle by the drive.

If chain driven, then the magneto should be secured on its platform so that the chain is just slack in any position of the drive. A chain which is too slack is liable to cause a "snatchy" drive, as the rollers will tend to ride up on the sprocket teeth, and this will result in excessive side strains on the magneto spindle. Where a triangular drive is provided from the crankshaft over the magneto and generator sprockets, particular care should be taken to see that the chain is neither too tight nor too slack, otherwise the magneto spindle is liable to be bent.

A Gear-driven Magneto

With gear-driven magnetos, the meshing of the gears is usually determined by the machining of the platform, but where adjustment is provided care should be taken to avoid tight meshing. A very slight backlash will prevent any side stresses on the spindle, and at the same time ensure quiet running of the gears. It is advisable to see that both the platform and magneto base are quite clean, as any particles of matter between the magneto and platform may tilt the magneto and cause either tight or slack gear meshing.

FITTING THE BOWDEN TIMING CONTROL

Having secured the magneto in position, the next step is to fit the Bowden control for the ignition timing adjustment. It is always good

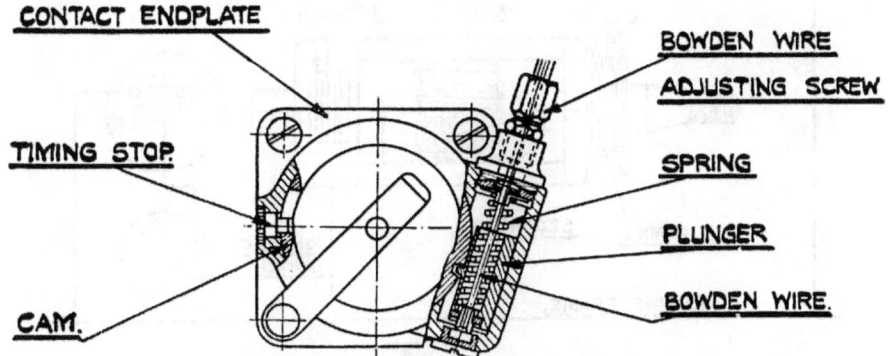

Fig. 4.—Spring-controlled Timing Arrangements on B.T.H. Magnetos.

MOTOR-CYCLE IGNITION

practice to first withdraw the Bowden cable from its casing and well smear it with grease, and then replace it in the casing before fitting to the magneto. This will not only ensure free and easy movement of the cable within the casing, but will prevent rusting for a very long time.

The Lever Type of Control

In the case of magnetos having a timing lever fitting on the cam ring cover tube and an overhanging bracket secured to the main body casting for the adjusting screw, first locate the nipple in the handlebar control lever and move the lever to the retard position. Next pass the cable projecting from the casing at the magneto end through the adjusting screw in the magneto bracket, taking care that the adjusting screw is screwed right down to give the maximum adjustment. Also see that the casing is properly located in the adjusting screw. Thread on the nipple which fits in the timing lever and cut the cable to the required length. This may be done by retarding the timing lever and cutting the cable just below the hole for the nipple. After soldering the nipple on to the cable, it can be located in the timing lever, and any slack taken up by means of the adjusting screw.

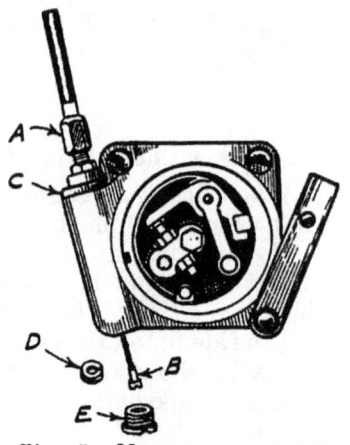

Fig. 5.—METHOD OF FITTING TIMING CONTROL ON B.T.H. MAGNETOS.

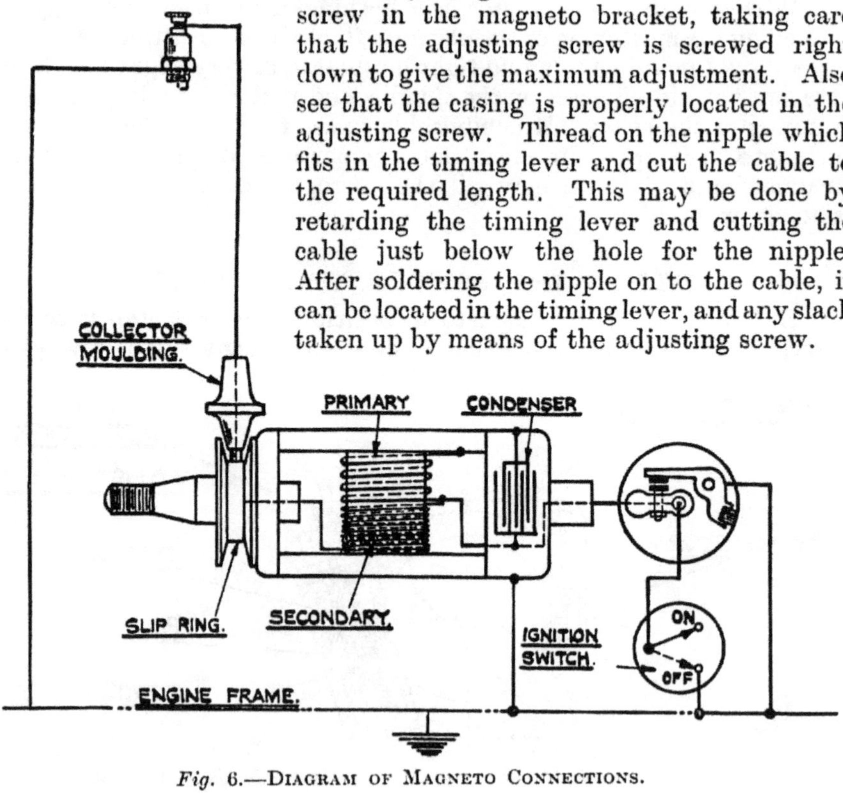

Fig. 6.—DIAGRAM OF MAGNETO CONNECTIONS.

MOTOR-CYCLE IGNITION

The Plunger Type of Magneto Control

The procedure for fitting the Bowden cable on magnetos with the plunger type of control varies slightly for different makes. Taking the case of the B.T.H. timing control illustrated in Fig. 5, remove the adjusting screw A and the screw cap E. Slip the screw over the cable and securely solder the nipple B on to the end of the cable. Replace the adjusting screw in the body C, screwing it right down for the maximum adjustment. Push the Bowden cable through the casing so that it protrudes from the lower end as shown. Fit the split washer D on to the cable and thread on to the nipple B. Then pull cable from the control

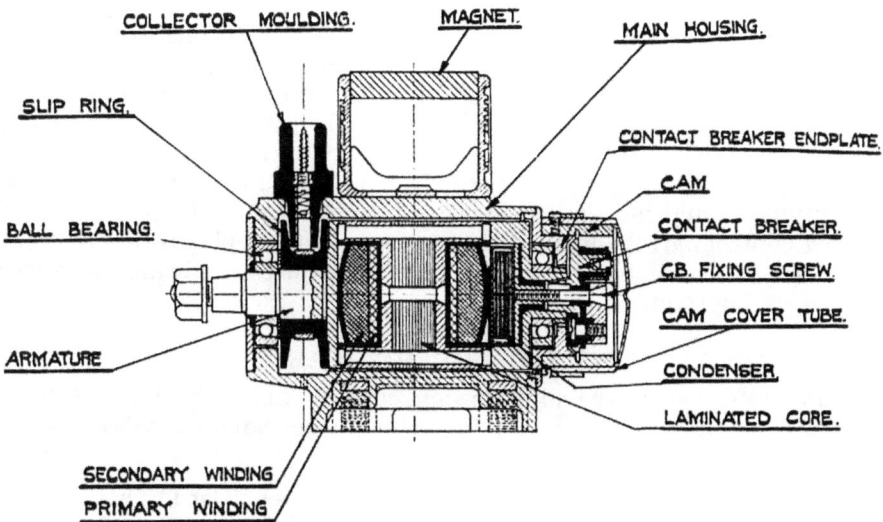

Fig. 7.—SECTIONAL VIEW OF B.T.H. TYPE K1 MAGNETO.

end until the nipple and split washer locate in the recess in the end of the plunger. Replace the screw cap E and fit the Bowden cable to the handlebar control, making the final adjustment by unscrewing the adjusting screw A.

Fitting the Bowden Cable to a Lucas Magneto

The Lucas magneto timing control shown in Fig. 8 may be fitted in a somewhat similar manner. In this case it is first necessary to withdraw the cam A and remove screw B, when the adjusting screw assembly, the spring and plunger may be withdrawn. After threading the cable through the adjusting screw and spring, the end is secured to the hollow screw H, which is fitted in the plunger, and all the components replaced in the magneto casing. The Bowden cable is then fitted with the nipple

MOTOR-CYCLE IGNITION

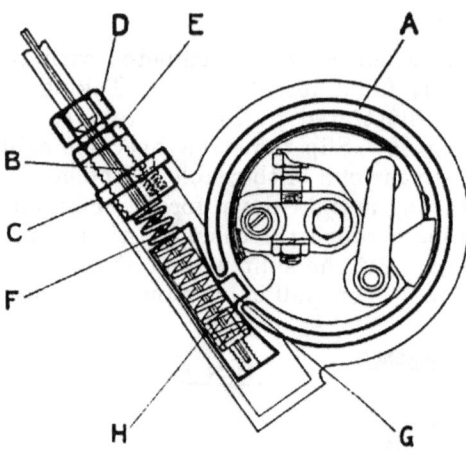

Fig. 8.—METHOD OF FITTING TIMING CONTROL ON LUCAS MAGNETOS.

at the handlebar end after cutting off to the correct length and the nipple fitted in the ignition control lever. Any slack may be taken up by unscrewing the adjusting screw D.

Removal of the cam and plunger is not necessary on " M-L " magnetos, as the nipple is located in the top of the plunger, which projects above the magneto casing if the cam is moved to one extreme position. After threading the Bowden cable through the adjusting screw, the spring control barrel and spring, and soldering the nipple to the end of the cable, the nipple should be slipped sideways into the top of the plunger. The spring control barrel and adjusting screw are then replaced, and the cable fitted to the handlebar control lever, final adjustment being made with the adjusting screw.

FITTING THE H.T. CABLE

On motor-cycles the high-tension cable is not only exposed to all weather conditions, but is also subjected to considerable vibration and possibly chafing.

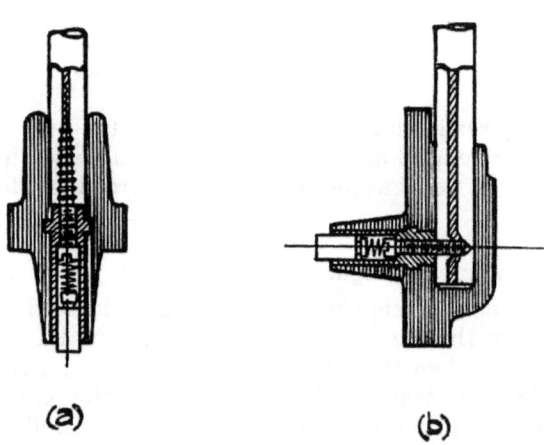

Fig. 9.—TWO METHODS OF FITTING H.T. CABLES IN THE COLLECTOR MOULDINGS.

Use Good Quality and Correct Size of Cable

Only good quality cable should therefore be used, and this should be 7 mm. diameter over the rubber insulation in order to fit snugly in the collector or pick-up moulding. Oversize cable, necessitating paring down to fit the collector moulding, should never be used, as it is very difficult to cut the insulation to ensure a good fit. If the cable is not a good fit, water is likely to pene-

MOTOR-CYCLE IGNITION

trate into the collector moulding, and this will cause misfiring.

The two general methods of fitting the high-tension cables are illustrated in Fig. 9. One method is to screw the cable on to a central

Fig. 10.—Lucas Type KR1 Magneto.

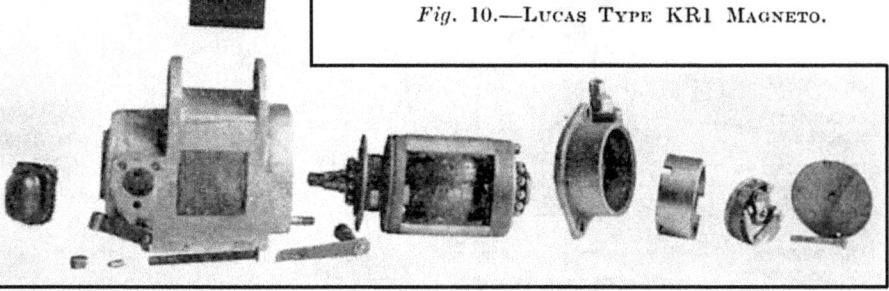

Fig. 11.—Lucas Type MA2 Magneto—Exploded View.

wood screw, which is integral with the metal insert forming the brush box. In the second method, it is first necessary to remove the carbon brush and spring and unscrew the cable piercing screw. After inserting the cable and making quite sure it is pushed right home into the moulding, the piercing screw is refitted and also the carbon brush and spring.

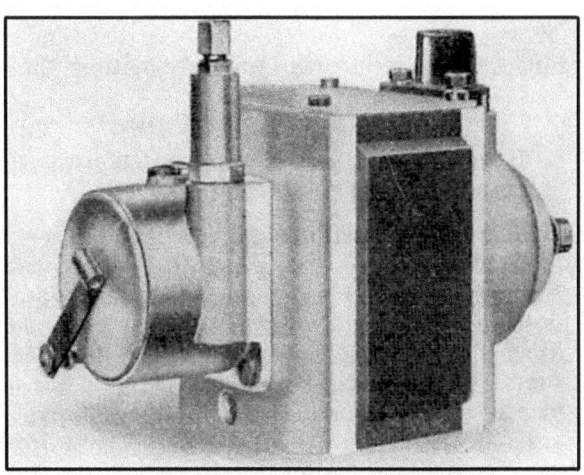

Fig. 12.—M-L Type CK1 Magneto.

MOTOR-CYCLE IGNITION

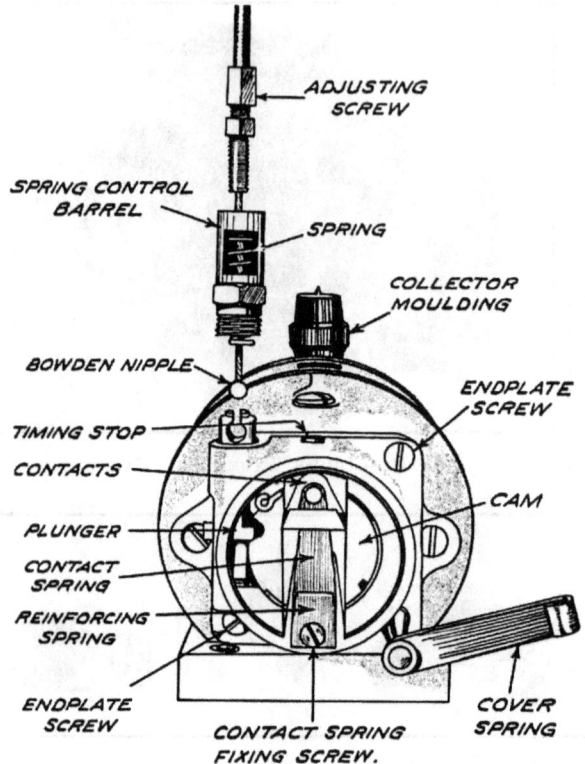

Fig. 13.—M-L Type CMA Magneto, showing Contact Breaker.

Adjusting the Carbon Brush

Great care is taken by magneto manufacturers to see that the carbon brush pressure is within certain limits, otherwise excessive wear of the brush and slip ring may result. It is therefore very important that care be exercised in removing and refitting the brush and spring to avoid unduly extending or damaging the spring. It will be found that these may be easily removed and similarly refitted, if when gently withdrawing the brush it is also turned in a clockwise direction. Turning the brush in this manner tends to reduce the diameter of the coils of the spring and thereby reduce the pressure against the side of the brush box.

TIMING THE MAGNETO TO THE ENGINE

To obtain the best timing position for the spark the engine makers' recommendations should be followed.

If Makers' Instructions are not Available

In the absence of any definite information upon this point, a general timing is 25 to 30° on the crankshaft before the piston top dead centre position, when the ignition lever is fully advanced. With an external flywheel it is quite easy to mark the flywheel corresponding to this position. If the flywheel is not accessible for marking, then the next best means is the piston position in the cylinder. First turn the crankshaft until the piston is top dead centre on the compression stroke, and then turn it *back* until the piston is $\frac{1}{8}$ to $\frac{3}{16}$ inch lower down the stroke. This will then be the piston position corresponding to the advanced spark timing.

MOTOR-CYCLE IGNITION

Set the Gear Wheel or Sprocket

With the sprocket or gear wheel loose on the magneto spindle, turn the latter until the heel is on the high part of the cam and the contacts are fully open.

Now check the Contact Gap

Check the contact gap to make quite sure that it is correctly set. A ·012-inch feeler gauge should just be a comfortable fit between the points. Take care that the gauge is quite clean before inserting it between the contacts. This is important, to avoid any dirt or oil getting on to the contact faces. Having checked the contact gap, now turn the magneto spindle back until the contacts are *just about to separate*.

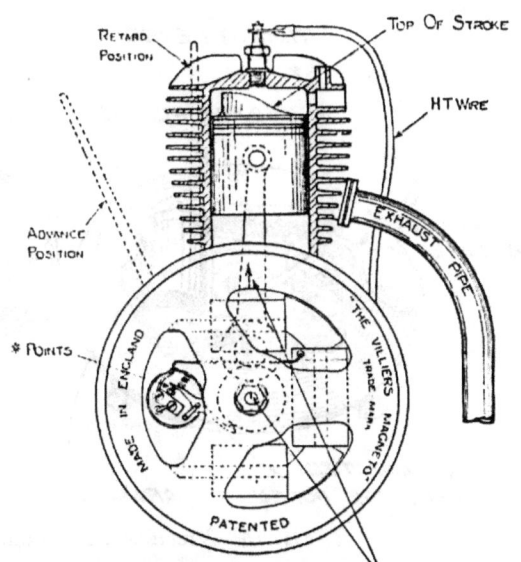

Fig. 14.—Illustrating Timing of Villiers Fly-wheel Magneto.

Tighten the Gear Wheel or Sprocket

Tighten the sprocket or gear wheel on the magneto spindle, making quite sure that the latter or the crankshaft do not move in the process of tightening.

Make a Final Check

As a check, turn the crankshaft round again until the contacts are just about to separate, and see whether the piston is in the required position.

In the Case of Twin-cylinder Engines

On twin-cylinder engines it is necessary to remove one collector moulding to see that the segment on the slip ring is opposite the aperture. The magneto should then be timed to the cylinder connected with the collector removed. In the case of "V" twin engines the back cylinder is generally regarded as No. 1 cylinder, and this should be timed to the magneto, so that the slip ring segment is under the collector marked No. 1 when the contacts are just about to separate.

MOTOR-CYCLE IGNITION

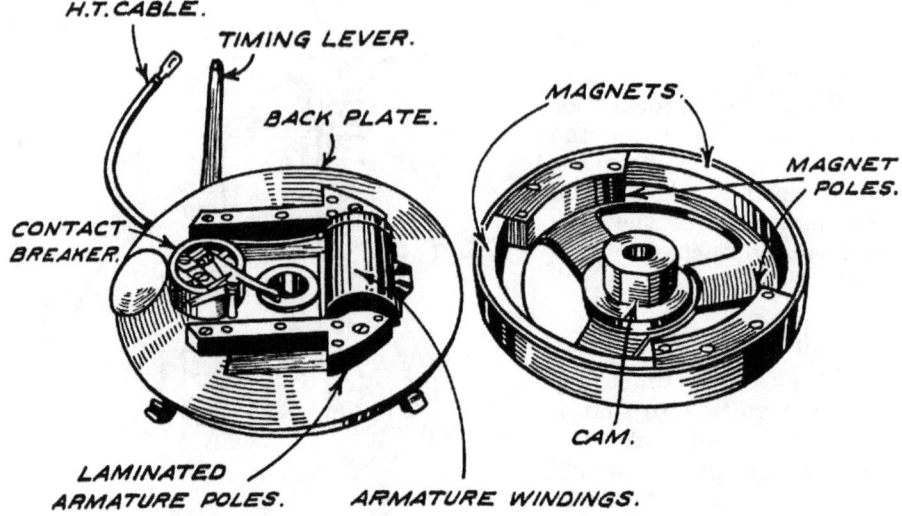

Fig. 15.—Villiers Flywheel Magneto.

The Villiers Engine and a Note on Flywheel Magnetos

To facilitate timing on the Villiers engine timing marks are provided on the flywheel and the engine shaft as indicated in Fig. 14.

It is necessary here to strike a note of warning in regard to flywheel magnetos. The flywheel should *never* be separated from the backplate carrying the stationary armature, unless facilities are available for re-magnetising the magnets or adequate precautions are taken to shunt the magnets by means of a piece of soft iron. The removal of the flywheel from the backplate without *first* bridging the magnets with a piece of soft iron will result in a permanent loss of a large percentage of the magnetic flux, and in consequence an inferior performance will be obtained. Motor-cyclists are advised not to separate these two members. If, for any reason, the magneto is required to be removed from the engine, both members should be withdrawn together. This may be done after releasing the set screw in the boss behind the backplate and, of course, after unscrewing and removing the centre nut fixing the flywheel.

How to replace a Villiers Magneto

In replacing the magneto, make quite sure that the taper hole in the flywheel and the taper on the engine shaft are quite clean and dry. Locate the backplate on the bronze bush of the crankcase and the flywheel on the engine shaft taper. If variable timing is provided, tighten the set screw in the backplate boss until the plate can be moved on the boss by exerting slight pressure on the timing lever. The timing lever should be approximately vertical. Next secure the flywheel by tightening the

MOTOR-CYCLE IGNITION

centre nut, after noting that the marks on the flywheel and shaft are in line as illustrated. With the flywheel in this position the contact points will be just separating, and if the flywheel is rotated clockwise until the contact breaker is opposite the next aperture in the flywheel, the contacts will be fully open. The contact gap should not be greater than ·016 inch, and should be quite clean.

The backplate of the Villiers fixed ignition magneto is located and secured by a steel strap fixed to a crankcase bolt.

HOW TO KEEP THE MAGNETO IN GOOD WORKING ORDER

The attention required by a motor-cycle magneto in service is actually very small; in fact, there are but few parts to which attention can be given. Nevertheless, periodical attention, little as it may be, is always well worth while, and will ensure that the ignition system is operating under the best conditions.

Fig. 16.—FINAL ADJUSTMENT OF THE CONTACT GAP.
Adjust the points so that a ·012-inch feeler gauge will fit comfortably between them.

Keep it Clean

Cleanliness is essential to the proper functioning of the ignition system. Exposed as the magneto more often is to dust, mud, oil and rain, a weekly cleaning of the external parts is always advisable. Particular attention should be given to remove grease or dirt from the external surfaces of the high-tension components, such as collector mouldings, high-tension cables and sparking plugs. Oil or grease on the high-tension cable will cause the rubber insulation to perish, and should therefore be removed with a petrol damped cloth. Mud or dirt around the collectors may cause the spark to jump to the magneto body casting over the insulating surface in wet weather.

MOTOR-CYCLE IGNITION

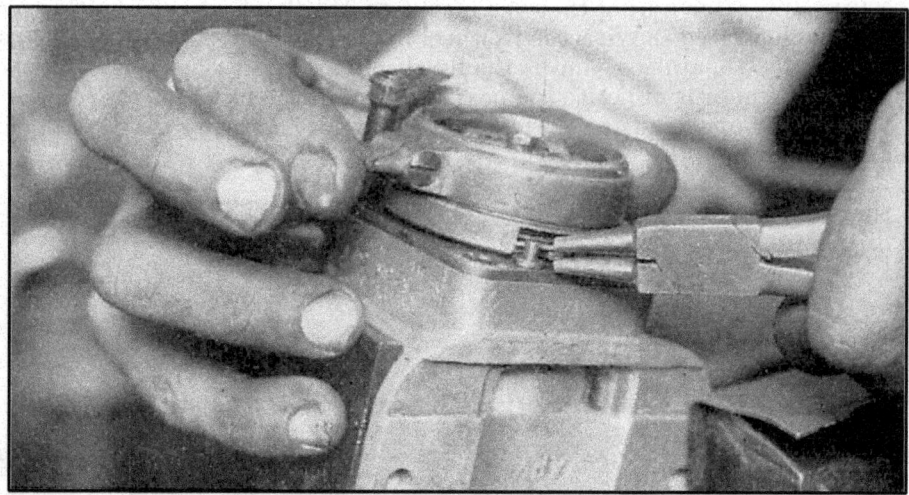

Fig. 17.—REFITTING TIMING LEVER CONTROL SPRING ON B.T.H. MAGNETO.

One end of this spring is located in a slot in the cam and the other round the timing stop pin. To refit cam assembly, partly fit it over the cam bearing boss as shown and with pliers pull on control spring and position round the timing pin. Then press cam assembly fully home.

Oil or dirt on the contact breaker points will prevent good electrical contact between the points, which is essential for the proper working of the magneto. Further, foreign matter of any kind is likely to cause arcing or flashing at the contact points, and this will not only result in misfiring, but will also rapidly pit away the contacts. Therefore any oil or dirt should be removed from the exterior of the contact breaker.

Don't Forget the Contact Breaker

All ignition units are designed to operate with a definite size of contact gap, and the makers supply a spanner and gauge for the adjustment of this gap. With magnetos, the contact gap is set to ·012 inch, and it is advisable to maintain the gap to this setting in order to obtain the best results. It is doubtful whether the contact gap will vary more than a few thousandths of an inch even after extensive running.

How to check the Gap

About every 5,000 miles this gap should be checked by inserting a ·012-inch feeler gauge between the points. If the feeler gauge is very tight or very slack between the contact points when the heel is on the high part of the cam, then adjustment is necessary. Slacken the lock nut of the adjustable contact, and readjust the contact

Fig. 18.—THE "CAMP" CONTACT GAP ADJUSTER.

screw until the gauge is just a comfortable fit between the points. Finally tighten the lock nut and recheck the gap to make sure that the adjustable contact has not moved when tightening the lock nut. Always make certain that the feeler gauge is clean before inserting it between the contact points. In the absence of a feeler gauge, the contact gap may be roughly checked with a cigarette card. It is, however, much better to use a proper gauge, which may be procured from the magneto manufacturers or any accessory factor at quite a low cost. In cases where the contact breaker is not readily accessible, the Camp contact breaker gauge illustrated in Fig. 18 will be found very useful. This gauge is designed with projections corresponding to the cam, and by locating the contact breaker on the central pin the contact gap can be readily checked or adjusted, and no further adjustment will be necessary when refitting the contact breaker on the magneto.

Examination of the Contacts

To examine the contacts thoroughly it is best to remove the contact breaker from the magneto. This may be done by unscrewing the centre fixing screw and then withdrawing the contact breaker. By lifting the check spring which locates in the contact lever bearing, and moving it to one side, the contact lever may then be removed from its bearing bush or pin, for proper attention. If the contacts are oily or dirty, clean them with a clean dry cloth. Should the contact surfaces be slightly pitted or blackened, they may be cleaned by means of a *very smooth* file or very fine emery cloth. Tungsten contacts are now almost universally employed on motor-cycle magnetos, and it will be found that these will give three to five years' good service before the contact surface becomes uneven. It is extremely difficult to true up the surface of a tungsten contact by means of a file owing to the inherent hardness of tungsten. Should the contacts be very uneven, then it is better to replace them, since the cost is quite small, than attempt to renovate the surface. Any discoloration of tungsten contacts as a result of oxidisation can generally be removed with very fine emery cloth. Platinum contacts, on the other hand, are more expensive to replace, and may be trued up in a lathe or with a smooth file. Great care should, however, be exercised to *remove as little metal as possible*, and to maintain the surface flat and square with the screw.

Always finally wipe the contacts with a clean dry rag, preferably a piece of linen, which is free from fluffy lint.

Before replacing the contact lever examine the bearing and bush, and clean these with a dry or petrol-damped cloth. Then smear the bush or pin with a little good light machine oil, such as sewing-machine oil, and replace the contact lever. For reasons already stated, it is of the utmost importance that any surplus oil is removed from the contact breaker. The contact breaker spring should also be cleaned and wiped with a cloth just *damped* with oil.

MOTOR-CYCLE IGNITION

Fig. 19.—A Test for Magneto Armatures.

In this picture we see how an armature is tested by an expert repairer. The primary is connected to a battery with an interrupter in circuit, whilst the secondary is connected across a spark gap set to discharge at about 9,000 volts. Armature OK if it sparks consistently at the spark gap.

Other Points to Watch

Next wipe the cam track and inside the contact end plate generally, removing any accumulation of dirt, oil or grease. Then very lightly smear the cam surface with a little oil or low melting-point grease. On most magnetos a small hole will be found at the bottom of the cam, under which there is a lubricating wick. Apply a few spots of light machine oil to this hole. Take all necessary precautions to remove any surplus oil which may be picked up by the heel and find its way on to the contacts.

When Refitting the Contact Breaker attend to this

When refitting the contact breaker to the magneto, make quite certain that the feather key in the contact-breaker base is properly located in the keyway in the end of the armature spindle. This is very important, as otherwise the key may be damaged, and the timing of the contact opening relative to the armature position affected.

Cleaning the Collectors and Slip Rings

The collector moulding or mouldings should be removed and the surface well cleaned with a petrol-damped cloth to remove any carbon or oily deposit. Examine the carbon brush to see that it is working freely in the brush box and, if necessary, remove both the brush and the spring

MOTOR-CYCLE IGNITION

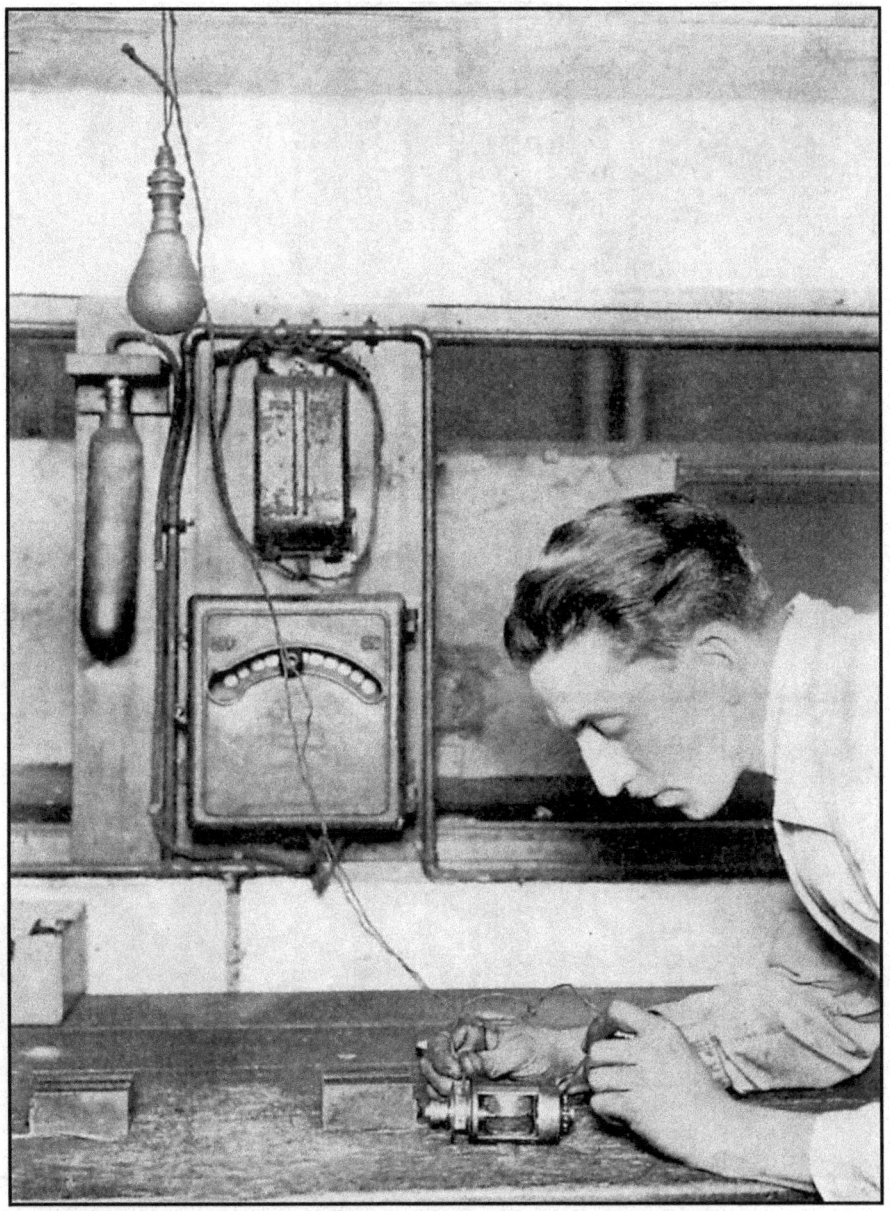

Fig. 20.—Continuity Test for Windings.
Supply mains voltage is applied across the ends of each winding with a lamp in circuit, to check the connections to the slip ring. Failure to light indicates a broken connection in the armature under test.

MOTOR-CYCLE IGNITION

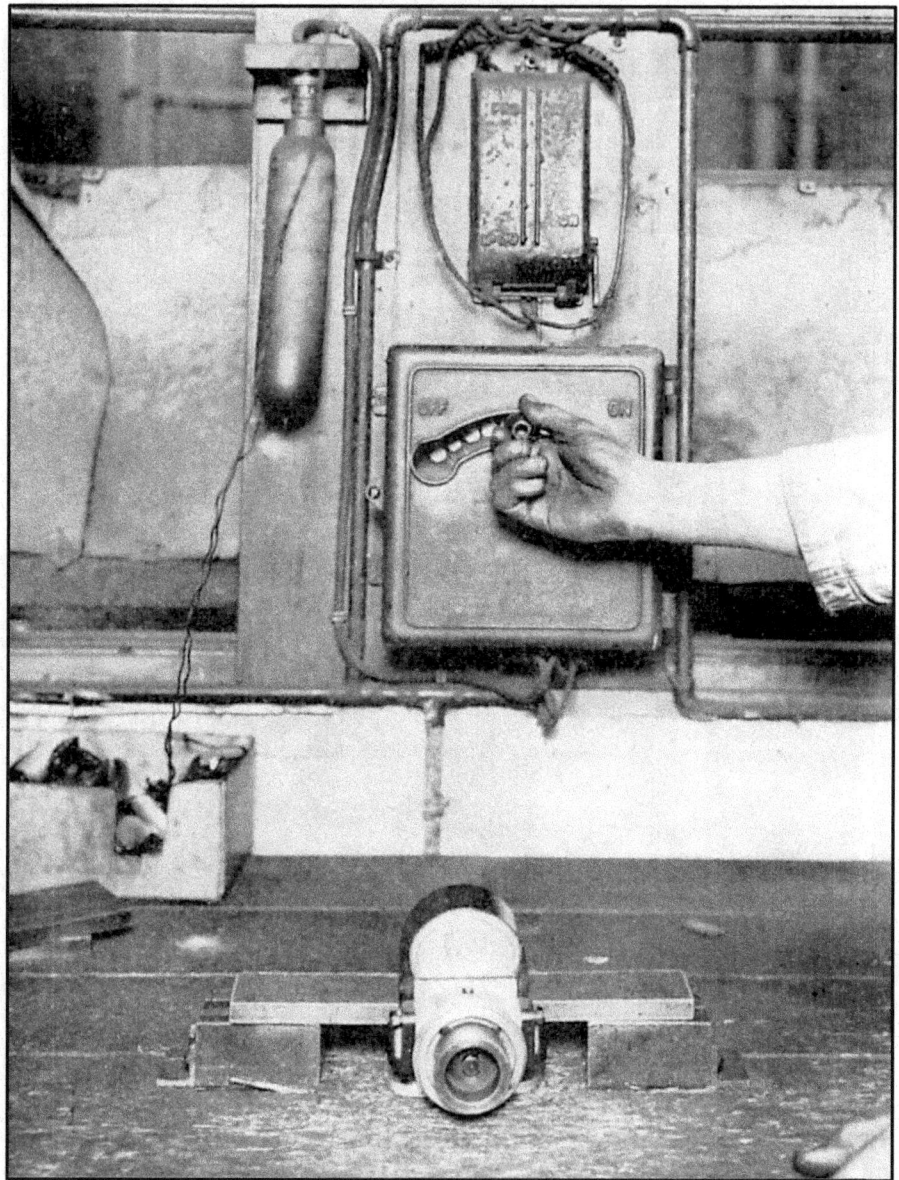

Fig. 21.—Remagnetising a Motor-cycle Magneto.

Whenever the armature is removed, the magnets should be remagnetised as shown above. A powerful electromagnet under the bench has its poles projecting. The magneto frame is placed alongside, and the current is switched on to the electromagnet through the control switch shown. Moral—do not remove an armature unless you are prepared to have the magnets remagnetised.

MOTOR-CYCLE IGNITION

and thoroughly clean inside the brush box. When removing and replacing the brush and spring, take all precautions not to damage or unduly extend the spring. If the brush is working freely it is advisable to leave it.

Never Oil the Carbon Brush

Any oil or dirt on the brush can easily be removed without removing it entirely from the collector moulding. Do not, under any circumstances, put oil on this brush, either to make it work freely in the box or to reduce wear on the slip-ring track, as this will only cause the brush to stick up.

Use Petrol for Cleaning, but remove Contact Breaker First

The slip-ring track and flanges may be cleaned by inserting the corner of a clean cloth damped with petrol in the aperture in the magneto casting for the collector moulding and *slowly* rotating the magneto spindle. As motor-cycle magnetos are not generally fitted with short-circuiting switches for the primary winding, it is advisable to do this operation when the contact breaker is removed. This will obviate the possibility of a spark from the slip ring igniting the petrol-damped cloth. Sufficient pressure for cleaning both the track and the flanges will be obtained by pressing the cloth into the aperture. The use of a piece of wood or a screwdriver blade inside the cloth to exert pressure on these surfaces is not recommended, owing to the possibility of damaging or breaking the slip-ring flanges.

Before refitting the collector moulding to the magneto examine the high-tension cable to see that it is tightly fitted.

The H.T. Cable—Don't be Penny Wise

Examine this for signs of chafing, cracking and perishing. The cost of this cable is not more than a few pence, and it is generally better to replace it if any weak spots are observed than run the risk of a breakdown which may cause considerable inconvenience.

The Sparking Plug—and Why Some Engines are Bad Starters

The sparking plug should be removed and the plug gap examined. If the points are worn the gap should be adjusted to ·016 to ·020 inch. Large plug gaps are one of the most common causes of difficult starting, and if excessively large may impose a severe electrical strain on the magneto windings and insulations.

THE SPARKING PLUG

Construction

A sparking plug consists essentially of an insulated central metal stem or electrode surrounded by an outer metal casing. The proper action of the plug depends mainly upon three factors, viz. :

MOTOR-CYCLE IGNITION

(a) A thoroughly gastight joint between the components.
(b) Exceptionally good electrical properties of the insulator.
(c) Good heat-resisting properties of the electrodes.

What the Plug has to Stand

When we consider that the pressure may vary up to 700 lb. per square inch, and the temperature up to 2,000° C., and that these variations will occur with extreme rapidity, we realise that the problem of sparking-plug design and manufacture is not easy.

The more usual method of ensuring a gastight joint is by means of a copper-asbestos gland, although in the case of the "A-C" sparking plug, the outer casing is shrunk on to the insulator by a special process to provide gastightness. Insulators are of materials such as porcelain, steatite or mica, which have good heat and electrical resistance properties.

Why Different Engines require Different Types of Plug

In order that the spark shall occur between the plug points, the distance over the surface of the insulator, externally and internally, must be relatively great, otherwise carbon deposit internally and dirt and moisture externally will cause the spark to leak away over the surface. The material and size of the electrodes must be such that the points will not rapidly burn away under the intense heat of the explosion or remain so incandescent as to cause preignition. On the other hand, the electrodes must not be too robust, else they will not get hot enough to burn off any oil that may be thrown on to them and the plug points will be fouled or shorted. Since conditions vary considerably in different engines, we see at once that a plug which is good for one engine may be totally unsuited for another type of engine. Hence the innumerable types of sparking plug to meet widely varying conditions. It will be evident also that great care must be exercised in the choice of a plug for a given engine, and the motor-cyclist will be well advised to follow either the engine or the plug makers' recommendations in this respect.

Examine the Plugs every 2,000 Miles

Periodical attention every 2,000 miles is advisable if the plug is to give its best performance. In the first place, the gap between the electrodes should be checked and if necessary reset. A good all-round setting is ·016 to ·020 inch, and generally the gap should not be in excess of ·025 inch. Plug gap gauges may be purchased for a few pence, and should certainly be included in a motor-cyclist's tool kit. Handy sets of gauges for plug and contact gaps and suitable for magneto and coil ignition are also available. The correct setting of the plug gap is important because oversize gaps require a much greater voltage to produce a spark at the electrodes. This will render starting more difficult; is liable to result in misfiring under full throttle conditions, and will, as

MOTOR-CYCLE IGNITION

Fig. 22.—Removing a Tight Slip Ring.
Use a drift gently as shown.

already stated, impose unnecessarily high electrical stresses on the insulation of the whole ignition system.

To ensure that the spark is not weakened through leakage, the insulator surface should be maintained reasonably clean and certainly free from deposit. Where the plug is of the detachable type, the gland nut should be unscrewed and the central stem and insulator removed. The insulator and the bore of the plug should be wiped with cloth soaked with petrol to remove the carbon deposit. It is a good plan to soak the entire plug in petrol for a few minutes, as this will facilitate removal of the carbon deposition. Do not use any sharp instrument to scrape the deposit from the insulator, as this will damage the surface and do more harm than good. When reassembling the plug care should be taken to see that the gland nut is thoroughly tight, and also it is advisable to recheck the plug gaps.

In the case of sparking plugs which cannot be dismantled, these may be cleaned by rubbing the insulator and the inside of the plug with a small screwdriver blade wrapped with a cloth soaked in petrol. Wire cloth can be used judiciously for cleaning the carbon deposit off the points. Finally wipe the insulator and body of the plug with a dry cloth. When replacing the plug in the engine make sure that it is screwed tightly home.

When to renew Sparking Plugs

Sparking plugs which have been in service for a considerable period should be replaced by new ones. It is difficult to state definitely the

MOTOR-CYCLE IGNITION

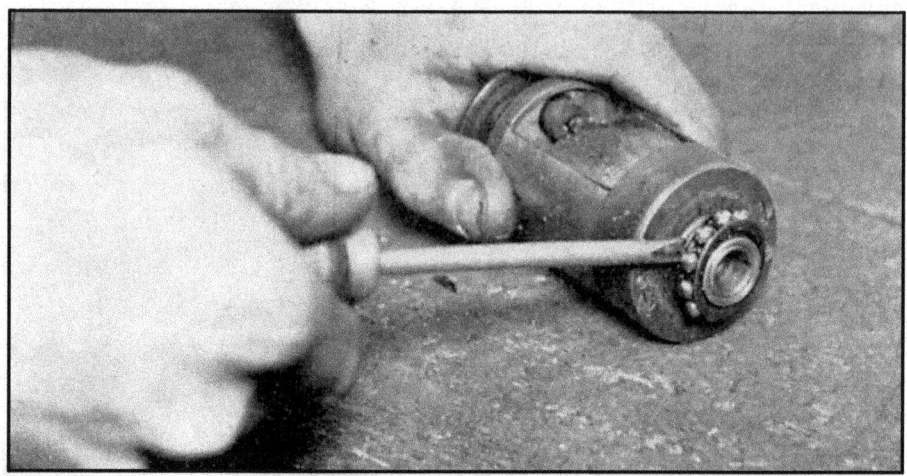

Fig. 23.—Removing Ball Cage.
This can be effected by judicious use of a screwdriver as above.

useful life of a sparking plug, as this depends so much upon the operating and service conditions, but 10,000 to 15,000 miles is a good average for renewal. In the absence of other causes, loss of power, poor acceleration and high petrol consumption are indications that new plugs are required.

Spark Intensifiers—their Utility and Limits

Spark intensifiers are sometimes interposed between the magneto and the sparking plug—usually as an attachment to the plug—in order to produce more definite sparking at the plug points. Except in the case of engines in which there is a tendency for the plug to foul or soot up, it is doubtful whether any benefit is derived by their use on motor-cycle engines. Since such devices consist of some form of external spark gap, either as a single gap or a multiplicity of small gaps, they necessarily increase the voltage required to be generated by the magneto. This increases the electrical stress on the windings, and will also increase the minimum speed at which the magneto will spark, and so tend to make starting more difficult.

The advantage of spark intensifiers, as they are called, lies in the fact that they serve to insulate the secondary winding from the plug electrode right up to the instant when the spark occurs. In the case of a very sooty plug, the current leakage that occurs during the time the secondary voltage is building up may be sufficient to prevent the magneto generating a high enough voltage to produce a spark. The introduction of the external spark gap prevents this leakage of current, and permits the magneto to generate the required sparking voltage.

MOTOR-CYCLE IGNITION

Fig. 24.—Extracting an Inner Ballrace.
This requires a special extractor, which is used as shown above.

TESTING THE SPARKING PLUG

The fact that a spark will occur across the plug points when the plug is removed from the engine *is no indication whatever that it will spark correctly when in the engine.* The voltage necessary to produce a spark across the points when the plug is in the engine is very much greater than the voltage that will produce a spark in the open air. Whatever tests are made then must be made with the plug fitted in the engine.

A Simple but Effective Test

A very simple test is to rest the blade of a screwdriver on the cylinder head and bring the extremity in close proximity to the sparking-plug terminal. If a spark jumps between the terminal and the screwdriver blade when they are 2 to 3 mm. apart, it can be concluded that the spark is occurring in the cylinder. Should it be necessary to bring the blade closer to obtain a spark, either the plug gaps are too small or the plug is leaky or fouled, assuming, of course, that the rest of the ignition system is in order.

Neon Tube Testers and their Use

There are on the market a number of inexpensive sparking-plug testers of the neon tube variety. Usually they are sold as a combined plug tester and propelling pencil. When placing the tester on the plug terminal a reddish glow will occur in the tube each time the spark occurs.

MOTOR-CYCLE IGNITION

If the glow is bright it is an indication that the plug is functioning properly, whilst if there is very little or no glow, then if the ignition system is in other respects satisfactory, it is a sign that the plug is either badly sooted or fouled. A weak spark is indicated by a dull glow of the tester.

A later section deals fully with the dismantling, repair and re-assembly of sparking plugs.

IGNITION TROUBLES AND REMEDIES

Ignition troubles are not always discernible from troubles due to other causes, and for this reason it is advisable to look first for the more common causes of engine trouble. When trouble does occur, it is so easy to overlook such causes as petrol shortage, water in the carburetter, air lock or obstruction in the petrol pipe, or the ventilation hole in the filler cap stopped up.

Fig. 25.—Removing an Outer Race.
Here again a special workshop tool is required.

Symptoms an Indication of the Defect

The symptoms are generally a good guide in tracing the source of the trouble. For instance, regular firing when idling and misfiring under load or when running on full throttle up a hill indicates that the ignition

MOTOR-CYCLE IGNITION

system is capable of producing a spark when the pressure in the cylinder is low, but not when a full charge is drawn into the cylinder and the compression is high. The generated voltage is either too low or the voltage required to produce the spark is too high, and probable causes will be oversize contact gap, dirt, moisture or carbon dust on the high-tension insulators, whether magneto or sparking plug, or oversize plug gaps.

On page 64 the more usual symptoms of ignition trouble and the most likely defects are tabulated as a guide when tracing ignition defects. In looking down the list of likely defects we see that most of these are concerned with the cleanliness of the high-tension insulation and the adjustment of the plug and contact gaps. If therefore periodical attention has been given, trouble is much less likely to occur, and if it does occur, the likely defects are limited to a few.

The symptoms revealed by ignition defects may be covered by three main classifications, viz. :

(a) Engine will not start or run.
(b) Engine fires irregularly.
(c) Engine misfires under load.

IF THE ENGINE WILL NOT START, this indicates that either the magneto is not generating the requisite spark voltage or the high-tension circuit is shorted. On twin-cylinder engines it can be assumed that the trouble is not due to the plugs or cables, otherwise one cylinder would fire. In this case, the contact breaker is probably the cause of the trouble, and should be carefully examined for very small contact gap, dirty or oily contacts, or sticking rocker arm.

IRREGULAR FIRING may, on a single-cylinder engine, be due to defects in any part of the ignition system, but on a twin-cylinder engine the defect will again be confined to the magneto if both cylinders are misfiring. Heavy carbon deposition on the plug or magneto insulation, or some contact breaker defect, such as a loose screw, are likely causes.

MISFIRING UNDER LOAD.—Reference has already been made to the reasons for this. If the misfiring is confined to one cylinder on a twin- or multi-cylinder engine, then the defect will probably be found in the plug or the high-tension cable for the defaulting cylinder.

Tracing Ignition Defects

Unless the symptoms clearly indicate the cause of the trouble, it is recommended that the investigation should be carried out systematically in order to avoid overlooking any part of the ignition system. The various parts of the system will be best investigated in the order they appear in the table on page 64.

MOTOR-CYCLE IGNITION

First Examine the Plug

Obviously the first thing to do is to ascertain whether there is a spark at the plug points, so we must test the sparking plug, either by the use of a screwdriver or a plug tester. If there is any doubt whatever, remove the plug, clean it externally as well as internally, and check the gap. Should a spare plug be handy try this in the engine.

It should be mentioned here that spare plugs should never be carried loose in the tool bag. Not only will they collect dirt and grease, but also the electrodes and threads are liable to be damaged by the continual vibration of the motor-cycle. It is best to carry them in a tightly packed box with the thread and electrodes well protected by a metal or wooden cap.

Next the H.T. Cables

If it is found that the plug is not the cause of the trouble, next examine the high-tension cable, and particularly the connections at the plug and the magneto ends. If may be that the connector to the sparking-plug terminal is gripping the rubber insulation, but not making contact with the strands. Pull lightly on the cable, and if it is observed to stretch unduly from the connector, cut the cable off close to the connector and refit. If the connector cannot be easily fitted, dispense with it, and carefully cut away the rubber insulation to expose about $\frac{3}{8}$ inch of the strands, and secure the conductors direct to the plug terminal, after twisting the strands tightly together with pliers.

Failing any improvement, examine the connection of the cable to the magneto collector moulding, and make sure that good electrical contact is made between the conductors and the cable screw in the collector moulding.

Also examine the high-tension cable for any weak spots caused by chafing against the engine frame or the presence of oil on the rubber insulation. Adhesive tape may be used as a temporary repair, but any suspected cable should be replaced as soon as possible.

Then the Collector and Slip-ring Mouldings

If necessary, remove the collector moulding, thoroughly cleaning the external and internal surfaces to remove mud and carbon deposit. Examine the brush to see that it is working freely in the brush box, but do not remove it unnecessarily. Should the brush be sticking in its holder it can generally be released by tapping the solid part of the collector, not the cone portion, against the side of the magneto. The brush should then be withdrawn and wiped, as sticking is due to oil or grease accumulating on the side of the brush.

Whilst the collector moulding is removed, clean the slip-ring track and flanges with a petrol-damped cloth.

MOTOR-CYCLE IGNITION

Fig. 26.—How Motor-cycle Magnetos are Tested.

Note the high-tension leads from the "mag." to the two spark gaps on the test board. A revolution indicator is being used to check the magneto speed. Modern magnetos will deliver a spark at very low speeds.

Fig. 27.—Slow Speed Test on a Magneto Generator.
Note the high-tension lead to the test board and the spark jumping the gap. The speed is decreased until the sparking ceases or becomes erratic.

MOTOR-CYCLE IGNITION

And the Contact Breaker

Should the investigation of the high-tension circuit not reveal the defect, the contact breaker should next be examined, cleaned and the contact gap checked as outlined on page 45.

Observe, in particular, the condition of the contact points. If the contact faces are covered with a black oily deposit, look for the presence of any surplus oil on the contact breaker and the cam. A black oily or carbonaceous deposit on the contacts may be due to petrol fumes. If so, it will probably be found that the whole of the contact breaker, and also the inside of the contact breaker cover, is coated with a similar oily black film. Petrol vapour is particularly harmful to platinum contacts, and the resultant carbon deposit on the contacts will cause extremely rapid wear. It has been known for a pair of platinum contacts to be completely destroyed after a few hundred miles owing to the presence of petrol vapour in the contact breaker housing. Although tungsten contacts are affected to a lesser degree by petrol vapour, its presence will cause blackening of the contacts, with a possibility of misfiring due to flashing at the contact points. Therefore, whenever petrol vapour is suspected, steps should immediately be taken to prevent petrol dripping on to the magneto by providing a shield or tray above the magneto, which will drain any petrol leakage *away from the magneto*.

Dealing with a Seized Rocker Arm

A seized rocker arm may be freed by warming the contact breaker for a short time. Seizure is generally due to the fibre bush swelling owing to the absorption of moisture, which also causes the steel contact lever to rust. When the lever has been eased, a little light oil should be applied before attempting to withdraw the lever from the bush or bearing pin. This will not only facilitate removal, but will prevent damage to the bush. It is not advisable to try and prise the lever from its bearing, but rather extend the period of warming until the lever can be removed with comparative ease.

Rocker arm seizure is not a common trouble nowadays, and generally only occurs after the machine has been standing for a considerable period, as after storing during the winter months. This trouble has been greatly minimised by British magneto manufacturers by a careful selection of the fibre; carefully chosen limits for the fit of the lever and the bush, and also special impregnation treatment of the fibre. More recently some manufacturers have discontinued the use of fibre, and in its place use laminated fabric board, the fabric laminations of which are bonded together with synthetic resin. Contact breaker bushes machined from this material provide immunity from seizure trouble, and also have excellent wearing characteristics.

MOTOR-CYCLE IGNITION

Removal of Armature not Recommended

If this investigation effects no improvement and reveals no defect, then the cause of the trouble is either due to insulation breakdown in one of the high-tension mouldings or a fault in the winding or the condenser. Examination of the collector moulding will have revealed any such breakdown by the puncturing or burning of the insulation. In this case sealing wax or even rubber solution applied to the puncture may effect a *get-you-home* repair, but it is rather doubtful. Nevertheless, it is always worth trying, as it may enable the machine to be driven a few miles if precautions are taken to close the plug gaps to about ·012 inch, and not to open out the throttle too far.

The removal of the armature to ascertain whether the slip ring, armature or condenser is at fault is not recommended, unless this is done by fully qualified ignition apparatus repairers, who have the necessary facilities for dismantling, testing and remagnetising the magneto.

The Reason Why

It should be pointed out that the withdrawal of the armature from the housing, *even momentarily*, will appreciably reduce the magnetic flux of the magnet, thereby rendering remagnetising necessary. This point is mentioned in case any reader should contemplate doing so in order to thoroughly overhaul a magneto. Even assuming that adequate precautions are taken to shunt the magnet by bridging the poles with a substantial soft-iron keeper, there is little that can be done to the armature in the way of overhauling, apart from regreasing the bearings.

A Note on Coil Ignition for Motor-cycles

With the wider application of electric lighting to motor-cycles there have been tentative efforts to utilise coil ignition. On the score of initial cost, there would appear to be a slight saving as compared with magneto ignition. The dependence of coil ignition on the battery is, however, a serious disadvantage on motor-cycles. Unlike car batteries, the motor-cycle battery is strictly limited in size, and is charged and discharged at a very high rate. Further, it is subjected to very severe road vibration, which not only tends to disintegrate the plates, but also reduces the effective capacity of the battery.

With coil ignition, therefore, special attention must be given to the battery to see that the electrolyte is frequently replenished by adding distilled water. The connections should also be regularly cleaned to remove any verdigris and regreased with vaseline. It is also important to examine at frequent and regular intervals the connections and leads between the battery, coil and contact breaker. Irregular firing may result from faulty or loose connections, as well as chafed or damaged leads.

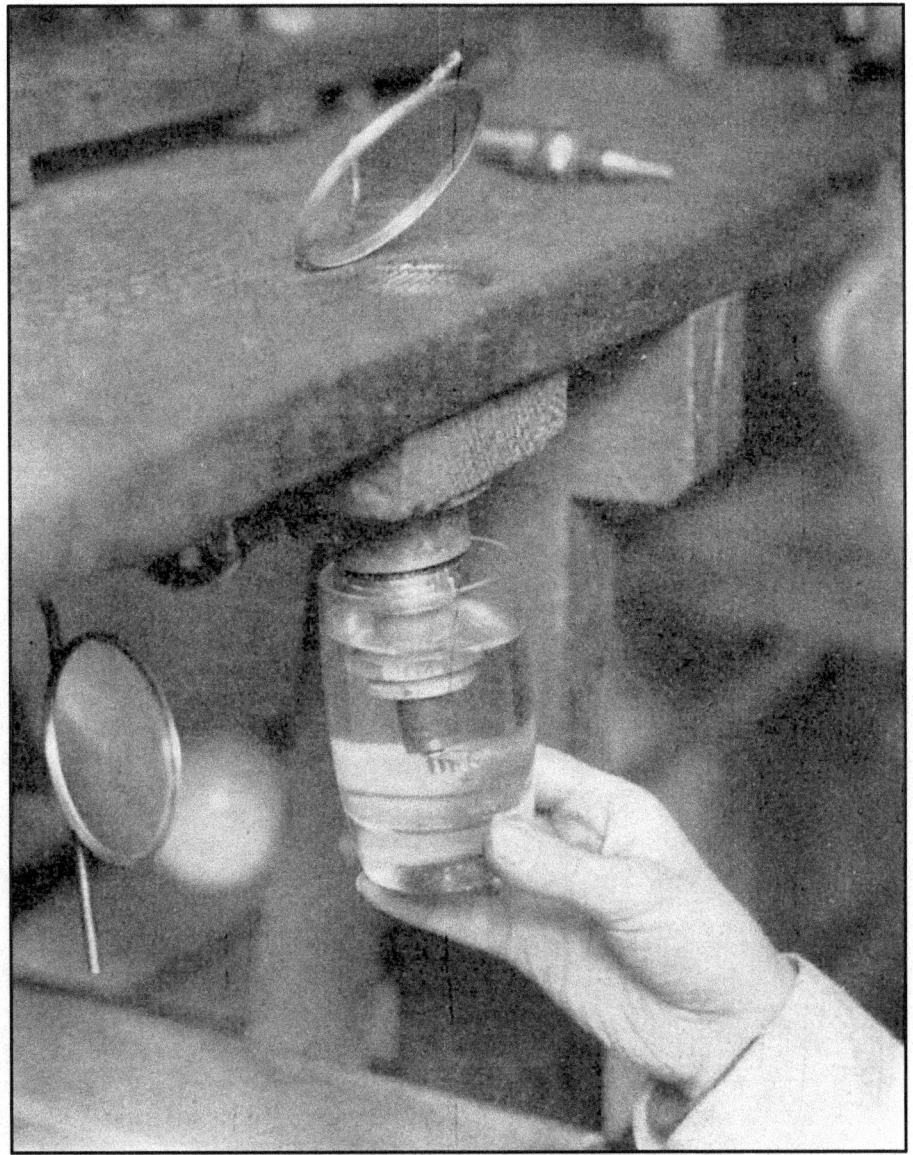

Fig. 28.—How Sparking Plugs are Tested.

This shows a plug being tested for a gas leakage. The plug is screwed into a cylinder, and is subjected, by means of compressed air, to a pressure of 100 lb. to the square inch. The plug, as will be seen, is immersed in liquid, and any leakage will immediately show by a series of bubbles that will rise from the actual leak, if any, to the surface of the liquid.

(*K.L.G. Sparking Plugs Ltd.*)

MOTOR-CYCLE IGNITION

IGNITION TROUBLES—SYMPTOMS AND LIKELY DEFECTS

Likely defects	Engine will not start or run	Starting difficult and poor low-speed running	Irregular firing	Misfiring at high speed only	Misfiring on hills	Misfiring on each cylinder	Loss of power at high speeds	Pre-ignition or back-firing
(1) Sparking Plugs								
Unsuitable type	—	×	—	×	—	—	×	×
Oversize gap	—	×	—	—	×	—	—	—
Dirt or moisture on insulator	×	×	—	—	×	—	—	—
Oiled or badly sooted	×	×	×	—	×	—	×	×
Cracked or faulty insulator	×	×	—	—	×	—	—	—
Insulator leaky when hot	—	—	×	×	×	—	×	—
Fouled or shorted	×	—	—	—	—	—	—	—
(2) High-tension Cable								
Insulation weak or perished	×	×	×	—	×	—	—	—
Strands broken	—	×	—	—	×	—	—	—
(3) Collector or Pick-up Moulding								
Cable connection faulty	—	×	—	—	×	—	—	—
Dirt, moisture or carbon dust on surface	—	×	×	—	×	×	—	—
Carbon brush sticking	—	×	—	—	—	×	—	—
(4) Slip Ring								
Oil or carbon deposit on flanges	—	×	×	—	×	×	—	—
(5) Contact Breaker								
Contact gap oversize	—	—	—	×	×	×	—	—
Contact gap small	×	×	×	—	—	×	—	—
Oil or dirt on contacts	×	×	—	—	—	×	—	—
Flashing at contacts	—	—	—	×	—	×	×	—
Contact screw loose	—	×	×	—	—	×	—	—
Rocker arm bearing seized	×	—	—	—	—	—	—	—
Worn or pitted contacts	—	×	—	×	×	×	×	—
Timing control retarded	—	—	—	×	—	—	×	—

Special thanks are due to Mr. F. G. Kirby of the Euston Ignition Co., Ltd., for his courteous assistance in staging the various photographs which have been used to illustrate this section.

Practical notes on the dismantling, repair and reassembly of sparking plugs as used in motor cycle engines are given in a later section.

SPARKING PLUGS
REPAIRS AND ADJUSTMENTS

IF trouble is traceable to the plug, or even suspected, there is only one way of dealing with it, and that is to remove the plug from the cylinder and take it to pieces. It is absolutely impossible to diagnose or attempt to rectify any such trouble in any other way.

A Useful Tool

There are several methods of dismantling a plug, but the quickest, easiest and safest way is by means of an ingenious little tool made by the " K.L.G." people, known as the " Quick Detacher." This comprises two spanners that act simultaneously on a worm thread, giving a 27–1 leverage that will immediately loosen the tightest plug, and ensure that it is reassembled to a degree of complete gastightness. The plug cannot slip during this action, and it is impossible to damage it in any way whatever.

The use of this tool is strongly advised, because it obviates any possibility of damage to the plug that is so often incurred when the conventional use of a vice and spanner is made. It is also greatly preferred to the use of two spanners, which action is most likely to bark the knuckles of the hand severely and damage the plug hexagons.

How to take a Sparking Plug to Pieces

Let us dismantle a plug that has been suspected of giving trouble. Fig. 1 shows a plug being taken to pieces with the tool mentioned.

Plug Troubles

The majority of plug troubles are invariably due to " sooting up," " oiling up " or " burning."

" Sooting up " is an accumulation of carbon that forms on the insulation of the plug itself and the central electrode, and this carbon forms a conducting party which allows the current to leak from the central electrode to the gland nut at the top of the insulation, instead of jumping in the form of a spark across the gap between the firing points.

Such troubles as this are, in the majority of cases, due to an over-rich mixture, and one should take the opportunity of giving attention to the carburetter rather than blaming the plug.

" Oiling up " is due to an accumulation of dirty oil and carbon on the insulation and the central electrode, which will either cause short

SPARKING PLUGS

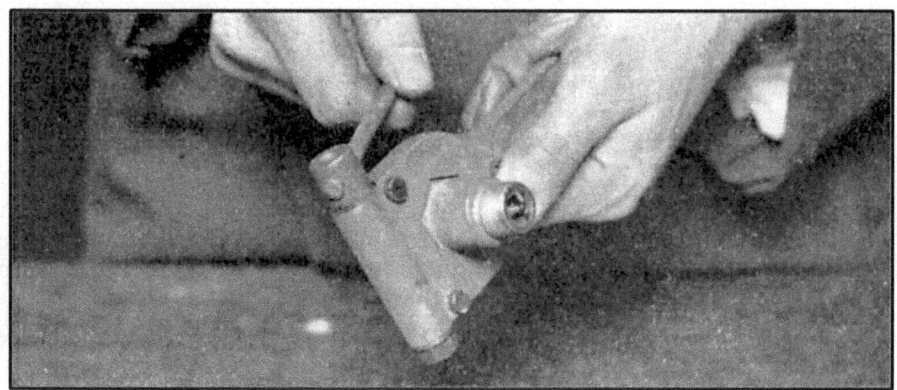

Fig. 1.—Dismantling Plug with Special Tool.

Fig. 2.—Plug Dismantled, showing Oiling-up.

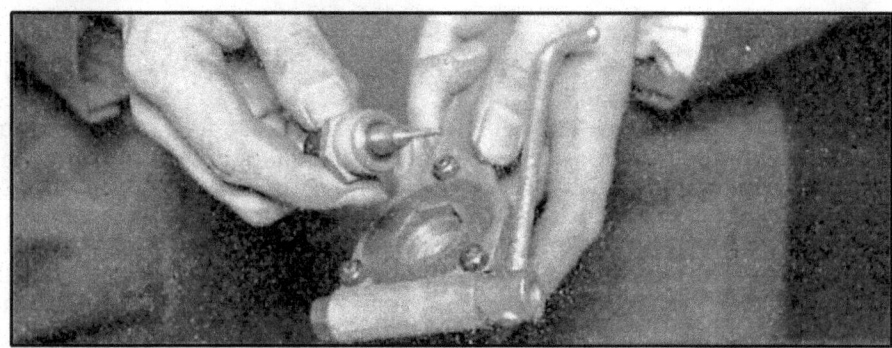

Fig. 3.—Reassembling Plug after it has been Cleaned.

Photos, courtesy K.L.G. Co., Ltd.

SPARKING PLUGS

circuiting from the electrode to the gland nut across the film of oil, or the oil will drip down the electrode itself and cause a " short " between the electrode and the earth wires.

It might be mentioned here that clean oil is an insulator in itself, but when a plug is " oiled up," it will be found that the oil is discoloured and saturated with particles of carbon, which make it a sufficiently good conductor to short circuit the H.T. current. Fig. 2 shows the plug that we have just taken to pieces, dismantled. It will be seen that this is in a very dirty condition, and it proves that this plug has " oiled up."

If your Plug becomes Oiled-up Easily

Before blaming the plug, the probable condition of cylinder and rings should be taken into account, and

[Photo, courtesy Lodge Plugs Ltd.]

Fig. 4.—DISMANTLING PLUG WITH HELP OF VICE AND BOX SPANNER.

Hold the body of plug by gripping the larger nut in the vice. Place, the box spanner over the gland nut and lever with the tommy bar. The centre should unscrew.

if there is reason to suspect that the conditions are bad, improvement may be effected by using a plug of lower heat resistance and consequent greater resistance to oil, for although one may clean the plug, the same trouble is just as likely to occur again after a few miles.

It will be noticed that the surface of the mica insulation of the present-

SPARKING PLUGS

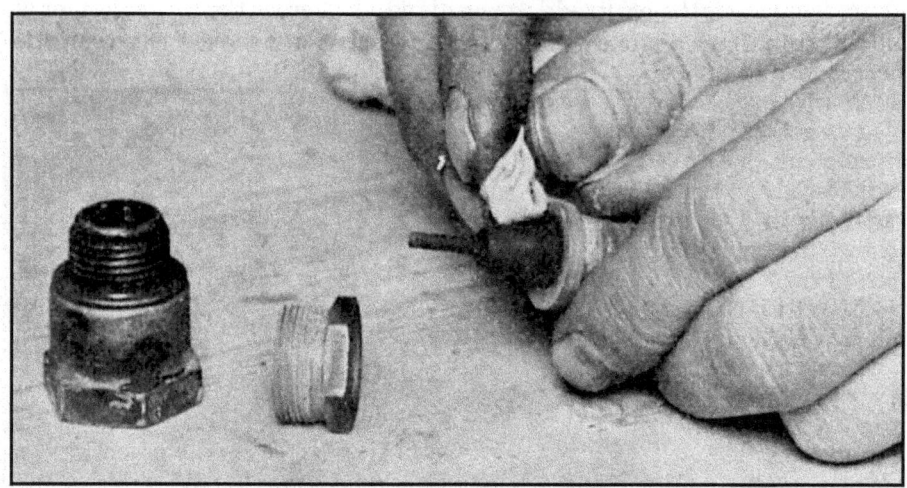

[*Photo, courtesy Lodge Plugs Ltd.*

Fig. 5.—CLEANING PLUG INSULATION.

This can be done effectively with rag soaked in petrol. In very bad cases of sooting or oiling up, it may be advisable to leave the electrode steeped in petrol for an hour or so before attempting to clean.

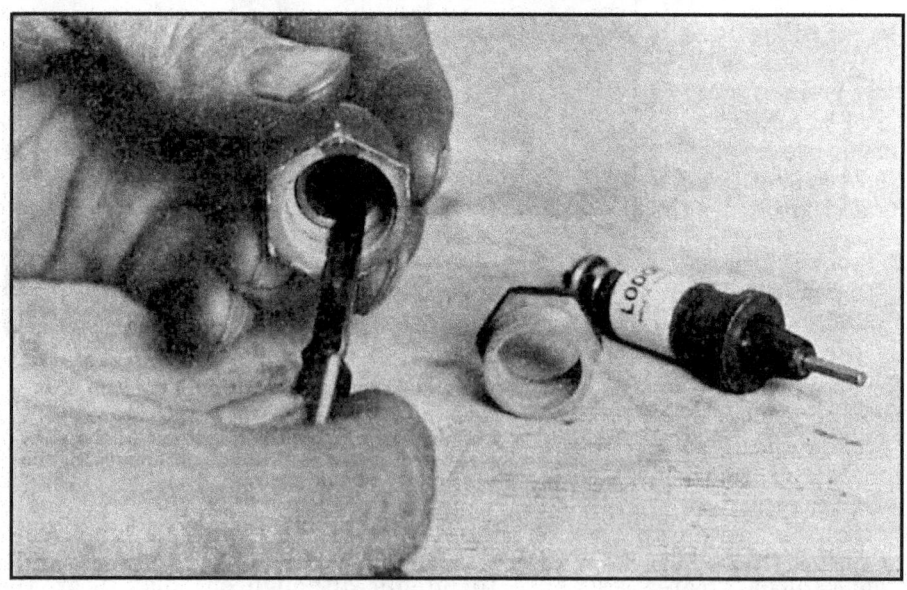

[*Photo, courtesy Lodge Plugs Ltd.*

Fig. 6.—CLEANING PLUG.

Scraping off carbon inside body of plug when dry after washing out with petrol or paraffin.

SPARKING PLUGS

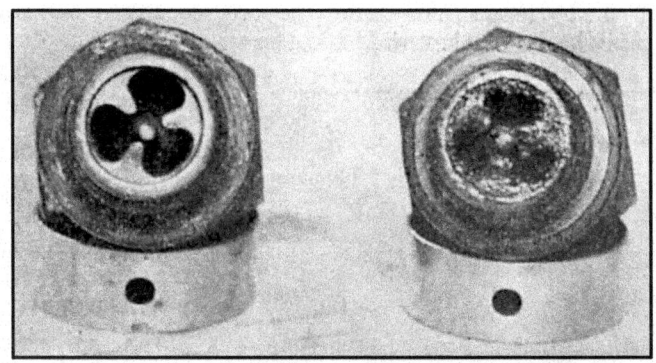

Fig. 7.—Two Plug Faults. [*Photo, courtesy Lodge Plugs Ltd.*]

Left, unequal gaps between earth points and central electrode. Right, sooted and oiled-up plug points in need of a thorough clean. Do this by washing in petrol or paraffin and scraping with a knife.

day K.L.G. "K" plugs is formed in a series of seven steps, and that each of these steps exposes the natural surface of the mica.

Cleaning a Plug

It is obvious, therefore, that in cleaning the greatest care should be taken not to damage the steps. In no circumstances must an abrasive such as emery paper be used. The treatment that is necessary can be carried out quite effectively and efficiently with a rag and petrol, although in very bad cases this may need a fair amount of perseverance.

A rag soaked in petrol should be carefully applied to the insulation, and by gripping tightly and twisting, it will be found that the accumulation of soot or carbon or oil will be gradually dispersed.

If the plug is in a particularly bad state, it may be found necessary to leave the electrode steeped in petrol for an hour or two, and then thoroughly dry, before proceeding with the cleaning method as described.

The actual firing point which is formed in a nickel alloy is not so delicate as the insulation, and the last quarter of an inch should either be scraped with a penknife or polished up with emery cloth.

It might be mentioned with advantage, that to give

[*Photo, courtesy Lodge Plugs Ltd.*]

Fig. 8.—Plug partly Dismantled.

SPARKING PLUGS

attention to just this part without taking the plug to pieces is of no use whatever, because it is the insulation which is the vital part of a plug and therefore needs primary attention.

Burnt Insulation and its Remedy

We have dealt with two main troubles that might occur with a sparking plug. It may be found, however, that the mica insulation is white and calcined. This indicates that the plug has been too hot, and that the insulation, as a result, has been burnt. It will then, in the majority of cases, be found necessary to have a plug possessing a higher resistance to heat to obviate this burning, although in some instances it may be due to too weak a mixture, and it might be advisable to give attention to the carburetter setting.

[*Photo, courtesy Lodge Plugs Ltd.*

Fig. 9.—TESTING GAPS WITH GAUGE.

The gaps between the central electrode and the earth points should be carefully adjusted to the correct measurement. The points should be moved if the gap distances are found to be wrong. Don't touch the central electrode. The gauge shown above can be obtained from Lodge Plugs Ltd.

The body of the plug should be well washed out with petrol or paraffin, and when dry, any accumulation of carbon should be scraped out with a knife. The three earth points should be treated in a similar way.

Particular care should be taken to see that the fragile and delicate surface of the mica insulation is not knocked against the body when reassembling (Fig. 3), and this applies when dismantling the plug as well.

The plug must now be screwed up tightly so as to make sure of a perfect gastight fit.

SPARKING PLUGS

Fig. 10.—How Plugs are tested for Firing under Compression after Manufacture.

SPARKING PLUGS

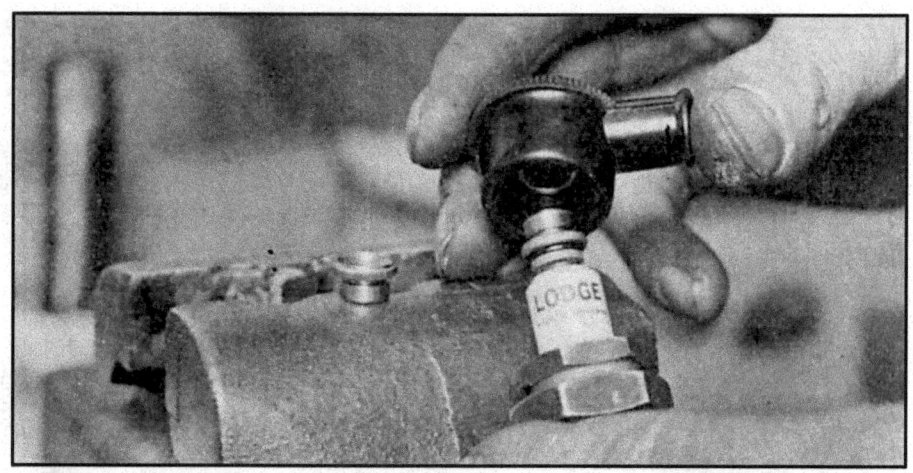

[*Photo, courtesy Lodge Plugs Ltd.*]
Fig. 11.—Fitting Special Waterproof Cover to Terminal of Plug.

Setting the Plug Gaps

Finally, the gaps between the electrode and the three earth points must be carefully adjusted (Fig. 9). The earth wires should either be tapped inwards with a small hammer and a punch if the gap requires closing, or carefully levered outwards with a small screwdriver to the necessary gap.

The distance of the gaps has a very considerable effect on the running of an engine, and they should be adjusted as accurately as possible to between 15 and 18 thousandths of an inch, if the engine is fitted with magneto ignition, and to between 25 and 30 thousandths of an inch if used with coil ignition. Preferably, a proper gauge should be used in order to check these measurements accurately.

Why it Pays to use Good Plugs

A large majority of plug troubles are directly due to an incorrect type of plug being used, and in some instances, through the use of practically unknown makes or second-hand plugs. It cannot be emphasised too much how greatly the efficiency of an engine is dependent upon the plug. One cannot pay too much attention to this little component, in whose power it is to make or mar performance.

Good plugs are well worth while, even though they may cost a little more in initial outlay. They will always well repay in efficiency and reliability and invariably yield a longer life, and work out at a cost per mile that proves to be definitely lower.

Most motor cycle manufacturers recommend certain plugs for their various engines. These recommendations will be found in the articles dealing with the respective engines.

ELECTRIC BATTERIES AND CABLES

AS USED IN MOTOR-CYCLE LIGHTING

By Edward Hill

Function

THE purpose of this most important item in a lighting equipment is to provide a reserve of current for supplying the lamps, horn, or other electrical apparatus.

Types

Three types of battery are in general use, i.e. :
(1) The lead-acid accumulator.
(2) The nickel-iron accumulator, as the Ni-Fe.
(3) The dry battery.

The last-named cannot be recharged, and is usually only carried as a standby on sets which do not employ an accumulator.

The lead-acid type of accumulator consists of two sets of lead plates or grids—positive and negative—immersed in a solution of dilute sulphuric acid and contained in ebonite boxes or moulded containers. The terminal voltage of a lead-acid cell is 2 volts, so that three cells are used on 6-volt sets and two cells on 4-volt.

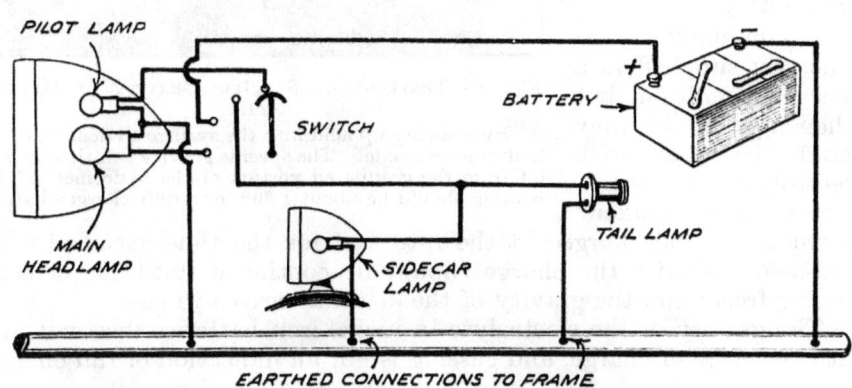

Fig. 1.—Diagram of Connections for Simple Battery Lighting Set.
Note that one terminal of the battery is connected to the frame which provides a return path for the current.

ELECTRIC BATTERIES AND CABLES

Each cell is fitted with a vent plug to provide for the dispersal of the gases generated whilst the battery is being charged.

The nickel-iron type of battery is made up of cells having a steel case, nickel positive grids, steel negative grids and electrolyte consisting chiefly of a solution of potassium hydrate in distilled water. When the cells are charged the case becomes electrified, and must be insulated from each other and any external metal parts. This is done by enclosing the cells in a moulded box. A stainless steel outer container may be fitted outside the moulded box. The discharge voltage of each cell is 1·2 volts, and five cells are generally used for a 6-volt system.

Special carriers are provided for accumulators which should be rigidly bolted or clamped to the cycle frame, and prevent any relative movement between the battery, carrier and frame.

First Charge

Accumulators are generally supplied in a charged condition, but when supplied dry they should be filled with electrolyte in accordance with the makers'

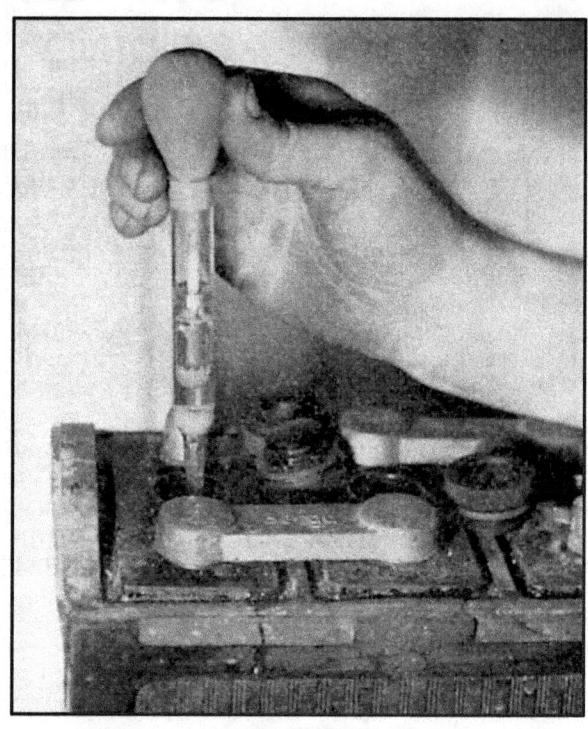

Fig. 2.—Testing the Specific Gravity of Battery Acid.

By drawing up acid into the syringe to float the small hydrometer inside. The specific gravity can then be read off from the graduated portion of the hydrometer. The reading should be about 1·300 for a fully charged battery.

instructions, and charged at the rate and for the time specified. For lead-acid batteries the charge should be continued until the cells are gassing freely and the gravity of the acid has ceased to rise.

The gravity of the electrolyte in nickel-iron batteries does not alter with the state of charge, and gassing is not an indication of full charge.

Maintenance

To obtain the best results from lead-acid batteries they should never be left in a discharged state. The electrolyte level should be kept above

ELECTRIC BATTERIES AND CABLES

the level of the tops of the plates, using only pure distilled water for this purpose. Terminals must be kept clean and given a slight coating of vaseline to prevent corrosion. Spilt electrolyte should be carefully cleaned off the container and the latter kept free of dirt and dust.

Cable leads should be well soldered in the terminal sockets and the sockets tightly clamped to the terminal pillars.

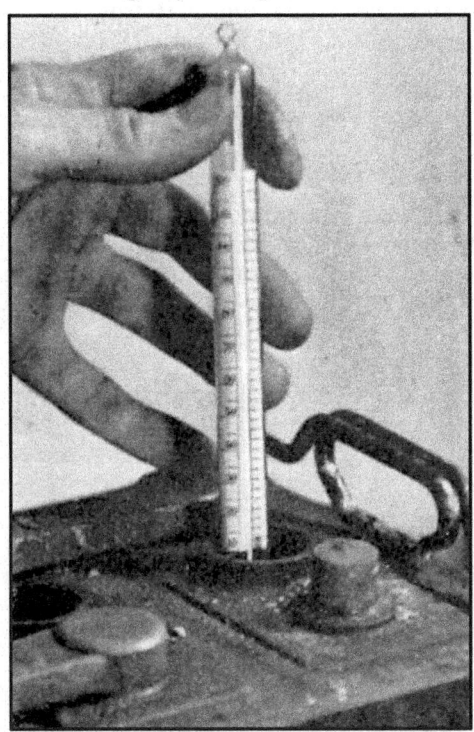

Fig. 3.—Taking the Temperature of a Battery during Charge.

This is a simple method of finding out whether the battery is being charged at too high a rate. The temperature during charge should not exceed 100° F. If it is found to be greater than this, the charging rate must be reduced.

No relative movement between the battery container and the carrier or frame should be permitted.

The state of charge of nickel-iron batteries is not of such importance as for the lead-acid type, as they quickly recover their normal condition when charged. The other maintenance points apply equally to nickel-iron types, with the added proviso that no trace of acid must be allowed to get into or on the battery or considerable damage is liable to occur.

The electrolyte of this type of battery must be changed entirely about once every twelve months.

Specific Gravity

The gravity of the acid in lead-acid type cells is a valuable guide to the state of charge of the battery, but it should be particularly noted that increasing the gravity by adding strong sulphuric acid will not charge the battery but will seriously damage the plates.

The actual specific gravity of the acid at various states of charge may differ with different makes of battery, but will approximate to between 1·260 and 1·300 for a fully charged battery, 1·200 to 1·220 half discharged, and 1·125 to 1·150 when fully discharged, assuming the temperature of the solution to be 60° F.

For nickel-iron type cells the specific gravity of the solution should normally be 1·190. This will gradually become diluted, and when it has decreased to 1·170 the battery will lose its efficiency and should therefore be emptied out and renewed.

Temperature

The specific gravity of sulphuric acid solution is affected by the rise or fall of the temperature of the mixture, and in checking the density a correction of ·002 must be made for every 5° F. divergence in temperature above or below 60° F. A temperature of 110° F. should never be exceeded.

The temperature of the solution in nickel-iron type cells must never be allowed to exceed 115° F.

Level of Electrolyte

It is essential that the level of the solution should be kept above the tops of the plates. The capacity of the battery will be reduced if any portion of the grids is exposed to the air, and the condition of the plates will rapidly deteriorate.

Topping Up

Pure distilled water should be added to the solution whenever the level has dropped to the top of the plates.

Spilt electrolyte must be replaced with solution of the same specific gravity as that in the cells, and the mixture thoroughly stirred.

Inspection

Timely attention will be well repaid by the prevention of breakdown. Regular inspection of the battery should be made at least fortnightly. The colour of the plates of lead-acid batteries give a good indication of their condition.

The positives should be a deep chocolate colour and the negatives a lead-grey colour in a healthy battery.

Top up as necessary and clean the terminals, then coat the latter with a film of vaseline.

Test the specific gravity by means of a hydrometer. Should one cell show widely different results from the others, the battery should be dismantled by an expert and the defect located and put right without delay.

Hydrometer Test

The hydrometer is an instrument which indicates the specific gravity of the electrolyte by means of a graduated float, after the solution has been drawn into the instrument. The electrolyte should be thoroughly mixed before taking the test, and it is advisable to make observations immediately after a run with the machine.

The float must be clear of the barrel and the bulb when taking the readings, and each cell should be tested in succession.

ELECTRIC BATTERIES AND CABLES

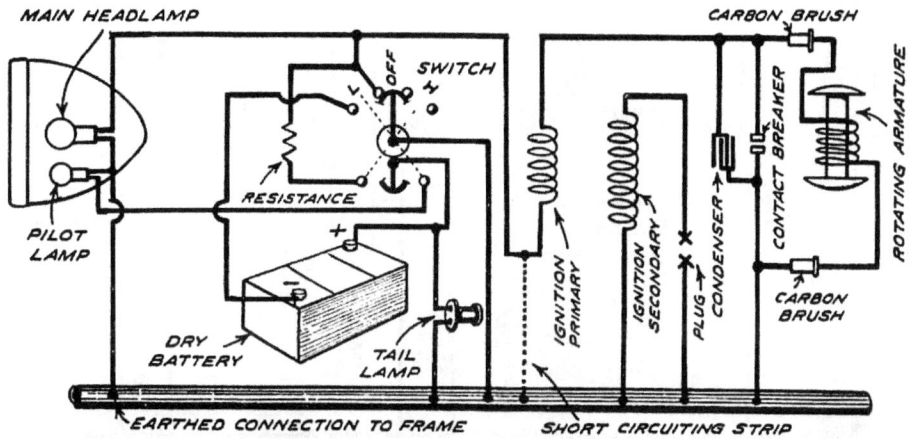

Fig. 4.—Diagram of Connections for Mag-Generator Set.
Notice that a dry battery is used in this system to provide lighting current for the lamps when the machine is stationary.

Faults and Remedies

General.—In all cases where trouble is experienced with the battery, it should be strictly noted that the accumulator can only give out what is put into it.

Charging must take place for sufficient periods of daylight running to store current for the periods when lighting is required.

More troubles are caused by low electrolyte level than anything else. Extensive damage may be caused to the plates when these are exposed to the air.

Another frequent source of trouble is vibration owing to loose carriers. The battery is of robust construction, but it will be rapidly broken up or damaged if allowed to shake about. The carrier bolts and clamps should be regularly inspected and tightened.

No trace of acid must be allowed in Ni-Fe cells, or the battery will quickly deteriorate. Test the distilled water used for topping up by means of litmus paper, before adding to the solution. Do not use any vessel previously used for acid when topping up. Rust spots on the steel cell cases are a source of damage, causing pinholes and subsequent leaks. The steel cases should be coated occasionally with bitumen paint.

Explosive gases are generated by accumulators of either type during charge, and it is dangerous to use a naked light near the cells for inspection or other purposes.

Wood or metal containers used for lead-acid batteries should be painted over with asbestos or other anti-sulphuric acid paint.

Electrolyte should be carefully handled, and rubber gloves should be worn when it is necessary to employ or refill cells.

ELECTRIC BATTERIES AND CABLES

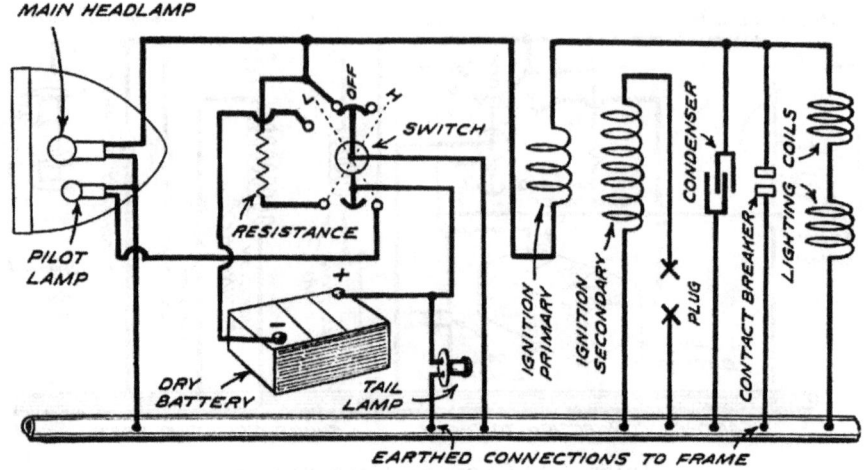

Fig. 5.—Diagram of Connections for a Typical Flywheel Ignition and Lighting Set. Here again a dry battery is used as a stand by.

Ni-Fe cell cases swell slightly during service, but this is normally allowed for in the spacing in the outer casing.

Defective vent plugs may cause excessive swelling, and on inspection the plugs should be blown through to ensure that they are efficient ventilators.

BATTERY FAULTS AND REMEDIES

Loss of Capacity. High Specific Gravity

Fault.—Level of electrolyte low.

Remedy.—Top up with distilled water.

Dim or no Light with Engine Stopped

Fault.—Battery exhausted.

Remedy.—Charge battery by making a long daylight run with charge switch " ON," or charge from independent source.

Dim or Flickering Light

Fault.—Dirty or loose terminal connections.

Remedy.—Clean and tighten terminal connections.

Fault.—Bad earth connection to battery.

Remedy.—Clean and tighten terminals of earthing cable. See that metal to metal contact is made by earthing clip.

Fault.—Broken connector bar.

Remedy.—Bar must be welded together or new bar burnt on.

ELECTRIC BATTERIES AND CABLES

Battery Exhausted or will not Hold Charge
Fault.—Specific gravity of solution low.
Remedy.—Charge battery. If not effective, renew the solution and recharge.

Electrolyte Leaking
Fault.—Broken cell case.
Remedy.—Case must be replaced. If the leak is visible a *temporary* repair may be effected by rubbing soap into the crack.

Loss of Capacity—Shorted Plates
Fault.—Shedding of plates, i.e. flaking off of active material or paste.
Remedy.—Wash out cells. Replace defective plates.

Sulphation of Plates and Terminals.
Fault.—Battery overdischarged.
Remedy.—Thoroughly clean the cells and plates—replace defective parts. Give long slow charge, then discharge and recharge at normal rate. It may be necessary to repeat the charge and discharge cycle.

Plates Grown and Buckled. Case Distorted or Swollen.
Fault.—Battery overcharged.
Remedy.—Replace faulty plates and cases. Charge battery. See that on long daylight runs the charge switch is " OFF " except for an hour or so.

Cell Reversed in Polarity
Fault.—Inter-cell leak.
Remedy.—New container necessary.

Dead Cell. Low Voltage. Battery will not Hold Charge
Fault.—" Shorting " between positive and negative plates.
Remedy.—Wash out cells. Renew electrolyte and any defective plates or separators.
Fault.—Shorted Ni-Fe cell cases.
Remedy.—Carefully separate each cell (except for connector bars) and remove any metal screws, etc., which may have become wedged between the cases.

Compound Cracked
Fault.—Defective sealing of cell lids.
Remedy.—Reseal with bitumen compound.
Note.—Do not attempt to apply any heat to the compound or to connector bars without first taking out the vent plugs and blowing away any gases by means of hand bellows.

No Standing Light. Dry Battery becomes Discharged Quickly
Fault.—Defective insulation of dry battery casing.
Remedy.—Examine fibre strips in fixing clips and renew any faulty insulation.

ELECTRIC BATTERIES AND CABLES

No Stand-by Light Available

Fault.—Dry battery completely discharged.
Remedy.—Renew battery—packing tightly in the clips provided.

Testing

For testing accumulators an accurate voltmeter is required.

This instrument should preferably be of the moving-coil type so as to obtain a deadbeat reading. Prong contacts should be attached to the voltmeter leads, and these should be pressed against the terminals of each cell in succession, the positive terminal of the cell being connected to the positive side of the voltmeter. Each cell should give the same voltage reading, which, for a fully charged lead-acid cell should be between 2·18 and 2·2 volts, and for a Ni-Fe cell approximately 1·3 volts.

To ascertain the relative condition of the positive and negative plates (lead-acid type), a test known as the cadmium test should be applied. This is done with a voltmeter, centre zero type, to the negative lead of which is connected a rod of cadmium. The rod is put through the vent hole of the cell between two plates. This has the effect of forming two cells, and voltage readings between the cadmium electrode and either positive or negative plate indicate the condition of these plates relative to the cadmium.

The readings between positive and cadmium vary between 2·4 volts charged to 2·05 discharged, and between negative and cadmium − ·25 to + ·2 discharged. Should there be a wide divergence from these readings in the results obtained, the group of plates showing the divergence is defective.

A rough test of any accumulator can be made by switching on the headlight, with the engine stopped, and if the light remains brilliant, and no noticeable drop in candle-power is observed for a few minutes, the battery may be assumed to be satisfactory.

To test whether the earthed connection is efficient, run a temporary cable from the negative terminal to the headlamp casing, and note whether the light is increased in intensity. If the additional cable increases the light, the earth connection is defective, and should be overhauled, cleaned and tightened.

The most satisfactory method of testing the battery is to have it fully charged from an external source, and then to discharge it at normal rate through a measured lamp load or resistance, noting the discharge current and time. The product of these items, i.e. current × hours, in discharging down to 1·8 volts per cell (1 volt per cell Ni-Fe) gives the ampere-hour capacity of the battery, and this should be approximately as shown on the battery label. A battery rated at 10 ampere-hours should therefore give a discharge of 1 ampere for 10 hours.

ELECTRIC BATTERIES AND CABLES

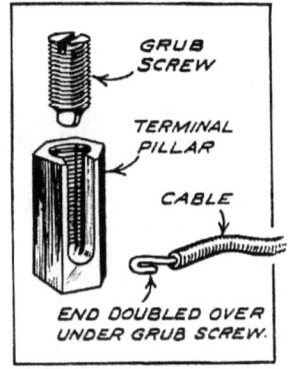

Fig. 6.—A Terminal Pillar.

The bared end of the cable is placed in the recess and the grub screw inserted.

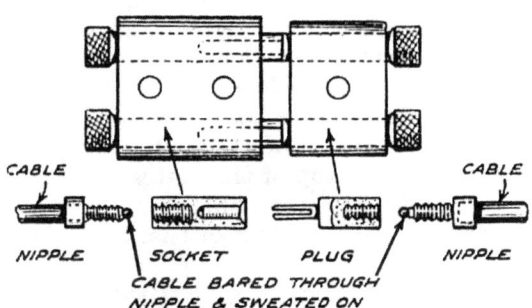

Fig. 7.—Cable Plug and Socket for Sidecar Lamp Connections.

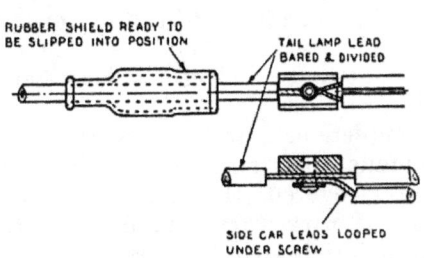

Fig. 8.—Method of Fitting Junction Box for Sidecar and Tail Lamp Leads.

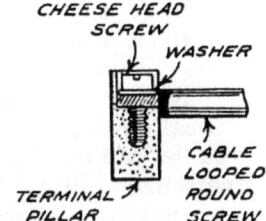

Fig. 9.—Another form of Terminal Pillar.

An alternative to that shown in Fig. 6.

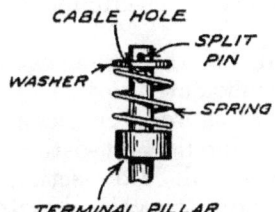

Fig. 10.—Spring Connector.

The washer is pushed down and the bared cable end is threaded through the hole.

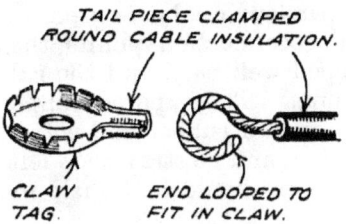

Fig. 11.—A Useful Fitting for Cables.

The claw tag is bent over the looped end of the cable and provides a neat terminal.

ELECTRIC BATTERIES AND CABLES

Storage

Should the motor-cycle be out of use for long periods, the battery should be disconnected and stored after charging in a dry, cool room. A boosting charge should be given the battery about once a month, and every third month after charging it is beneficial to discharge the battery at the normal rate, afterwards recharging without delay.

The electrolyte must not be emptied out, and should be kept above the level of the top of the plates.

Ni-Fe-type cells can be stored almost indefinitely, providing the battery is charged and then half discharged before storing.

CABLES, JUNCTION BOXES, ETC.

Cables are provided as conductors of electrical current from the generator and battery to the lamps, horn or other electrical apparatus. The conductors are covered with a dielectric or insulation, except at the terminal ends, so as to prevent leakage of the current between the terminal points. Leads should be as short as can conveniently be arranged, to avoid drop in voltage owing to the resistance of the conductors. Short bends should be avoided, and sufficient slack left at points where relative movement takes place between parts of the motor-cycle, so that no drag on the cable occurs. The various diagrams included in this publication show clearly the layout and connections between the electrical units on most makes of motor-cycles.

Cables are usually made up in complete sets and harnessed together by cotton braiding. Each cable is made up of stranded flexible copper wires, preferably tinned, single cotton covered (this may be omitted), covered with rubber, vulcanised, taped with varnished cambric tape, cotton braided and compounded or painted with oil-, fire- and water-resisting compound. The sizes of cores in common use are: $14/\cdot012$, $16/\cdot012$, $23/\cdot0076$ and $23/\cdot012$ inch.

The cotton or rubber covering may be coloured, or coloured sleeving may be used at the ends of the cable to indicate the circuit on which any particular cable is used.

For connection points the outer covering of the cable should be stripped well back and the rubber stripped sufficiently to just clear the terminal. The exposed copper core should be thoroughly cleaned and quite free of rubber and cotton. The strands should be twisted tightly together, and no stray ends left outside the terminal. Connections fixed by screws should be tightly made and care taken to avoid shearing the strands.

When a cable is fixed directly under a pointed screw it is good practice to solder the end of the cable so that the screw digs into the solder. Cables sweated to tags should be pushed through the socket of the tag, and the extruding end bent over and soldered to the outside of the tag,

ELECTRIC BATTERIES AND CABLES

leaving the entering end free of solder and retaining its flexibility. The cable leads should be cleated a short distance away from terminal points to prevent abrasion or damage by relative movement between the frame and the cable.

When disconnected for any reason, cable ends should be clearly labelled so that the correct reconnection can be made without difficulty. Terminals must be kept clean and tight.

Faults and Remedies

Almost all faults in cables are due to breakage, frayed ends or damaged insulation caused by vibration. Terminals and cleats should therefore be carefully inspected and tightened periodically, and any defective insulation made good by sleeving or taping.

No Lights. Dynamo Overheated. Bulbs Blackened or Burnt.
Fault.—Broken battery lead.
Remedy.—Trace breakage and renew or repair cable.

No Charge to Battery. Dynamo and Cable Overheated.
Fault.—Broken dynamo main lead.
Remedy.—Trace fault and renew or repair as necessary.

No Charge to Battery. Battery Run Down.
Fault.—Broken dynamo shunt lead.
Remedy.—Trace break and renew or repair.

Breaks in cables may be temporarily repaired by stripping the insulation at the fracture and twisting the two ends tightly together, covering the joint by rubber tape or sleeving.

No Light on Broken Lamp Circuit.
Fault.—Broken lamp cable.
Remedy.—Trace breakage and repair or renew cable.

No Light on Circuit Affected. Cable Overheated. Battery Run Down. No Charge.
Fault.—Short-circuited cable.
Remedy.—Trace defect, look for chafed cable, overtightened cleats, frayed ends of wires and cable nipped by frame.

After repairing, test to ascertain that short has been cleared.

Testing

Simple tests by means of a test lamp on any mains circuit are sufficient to ascertain whether the cables on a motor-cycle equipment are satisfactory.

Disconnect all cables at terminal ends, and test each cable for continuity by connecting the two ends to the prod leads of the test lamp. Test insulation by connecting one end of each cable to one prod lead and the other prod lead to a bright metal part of the frame.

ELECTRIC LAMPS
INCLUDING NOTES ON SWITCHES AND INSTRUMENTS

By Edward Hill

HEADLAMPS may be plain lighting units with a single bulb, and with base or side stud mountings.

More recent practice has introduced a number of variations, such as the following :

(1) Double filament bulb—one of high candle-power for night driving and one of low candle-power as standing light.

(2) Single filament high candle-power bulb for driving light, and separate low candle-power pilot bulb for use when standing.

(3) Double filament bulb—one of high candle-power for a headlight, and a second filament of equal or lower candle-power set at an angle so as to throw a deflected beam downwards when passing, and with a pilot bulb of low candle-power for standing light.

(4) Switch mounted on the body of the lamp for controlling the lights and in some instances also controlling the dynamo output.

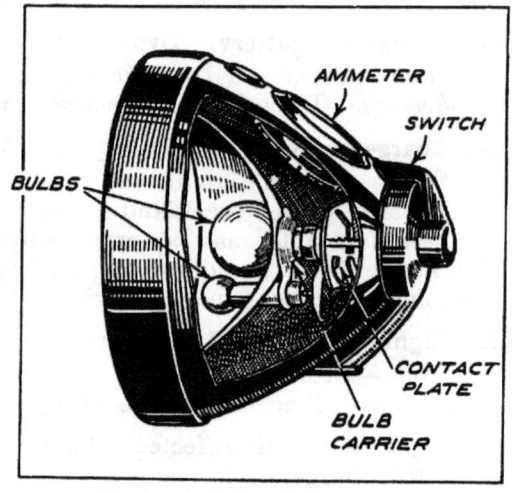

Fig. 1.—A Typical Headlamp.
Showing the pilot bulb and the arrangement of the switch and ammeter.

(5) Combined ammeter and rotary switch mounted on the back of the lamp.

(6) Ammeter and switch in separate units mounted on the lamp.

(7) Provision for illuminating the ammeter.

Both bracket and base mountings provide adjustment for setting the lamp position.

The headlamp—apart from switch and ammeter—consists of a body or lantern to which the bracket mountings are fixed, a reflector, lamp holders, detachable rim and glass front.

ELECTRIC LAMPS

The detachable rim is usually fixed by some form of bayonet fitting, and can be detached by pressing the front farther over the body, giving the rim a rotary movement as far as the bayonet slots will allow, and then withdrawing the front.

In some instances a screw must be removed before the rim can be given the rotary movement. Another form of fixing has a hinged bolt attached to the rim, which engages with a slotted lug on the body. A form of spring fixing is sometimes used, in which the rim is sprung over a slotted beading projecting from the body. This type is released by turning a cam operated by a slotted stud.

The fixing of the glass lens is done in a variety of ways. It may be spun into the front rim by means of an aluminium bezel, or held in place by spring clips, or pressed against the rim by spring plungers mounted in the body. In most instances a rubber ring is interposed between the rim and the lens to effect a watertight joint.

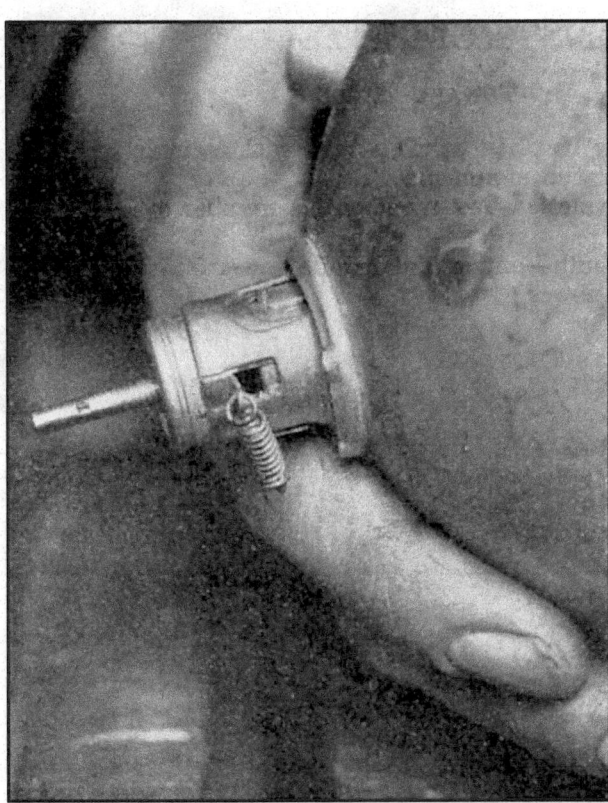

*Fig. 2.—*Showing Focusing Arrangement.
Note the grooves and the controlling spring
(Miller and Villiers).

In the older types of headlamps the reflector is held by an extension of the lamp holder projecting through the lamp body at the back and locked by a wing or knurled nut.

This method provides a very simple form of focusing adjustment.

By releasing the nut the bulb holder can be moved back or forward until the best position is obtained and refixed by tightening the nut. A

ELECTRIC LAMPS

Fig. 3.—A B.T.H. Headlamp Dismantled.

The interior part of the switch, fitted to which can be seen the ammeter and resistance, can be removed as one unit. The external part of the switch in the left hand shows the ball plunger contacts.

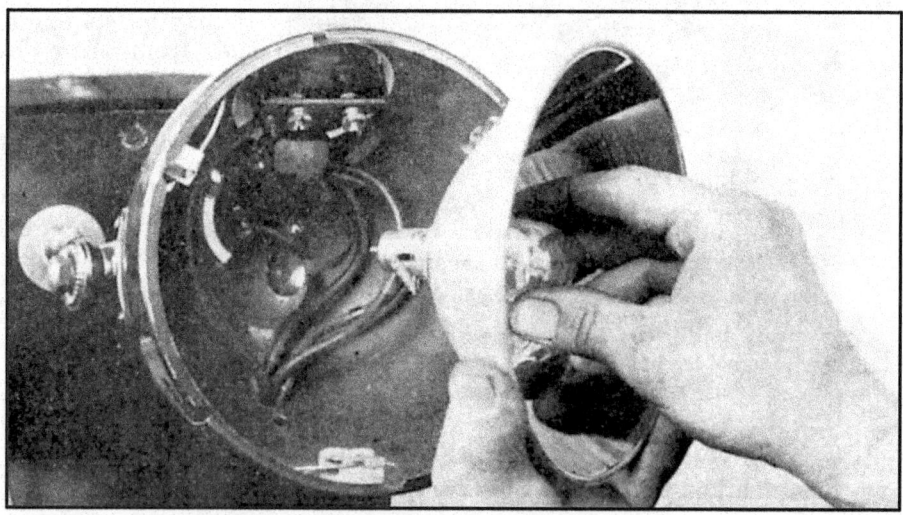

Fig. 4.—Inserting New Main Bulb and adjusting Focus in "Miller" Headlamp.
Note the one-sided toothed slot and retaining spiral spring at the rear of the reflector. This device admits of the correct focusing of almost any type of bulb.

ELECTRIC LAMPS

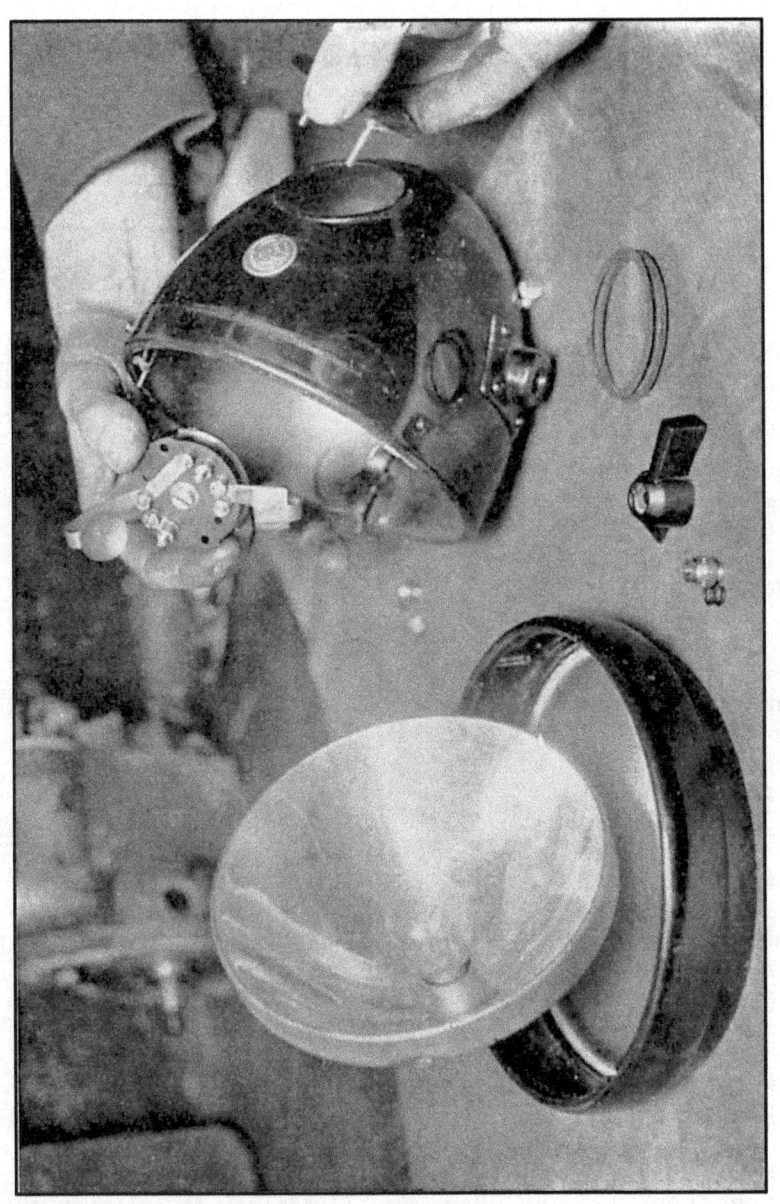

Fig. 5.—Dismantling a Villiers Headlamp.

ELECTRIC LAMPS

bayonet or screwed adapter is attached to the projecting holder to provide means for connecting the cable leads.

Later methods of fixing the reflector are by means of a rim on the reflector held by spring pressure between the body and the front, or by a rim fixed with screws or bayonet pins to lugs inside the body.

For single-filament bulbs a form of holder providing three positions in the bayonet slots may be used for focusing.

For double-filament bulbs it is necessary to keep the filaments in a set relation to the lamp mounting, and focusing may be effected by loosening a clamping screw and sliding the holder back or forward as required. Another similar method has the sliding motion controlled by a spring detent pressing into one of a series of grooves cut across the lampholder body. Pushing the bulb will spring the detent out of one groove into the next and give a different focal position (Fig. 2). Still another form requires a rotary motion to the holder, which moves the holder back or forward by a screw thread until the desired position is obtained.

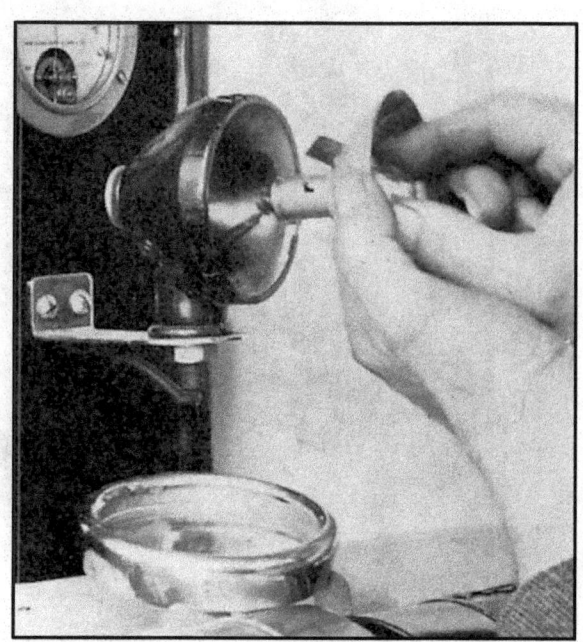

Fig. 6.—Fitting New Bulb in the Sidecar Lamp after removing Detachable Front (Miller).

Complete turns (with double filament bulb) are necessary, so as to reset the bulb in the correct filament position, and a spring catch may be provided to give this location. Cable leads are attached by a variety of means. In very recent models, cables inside the lamp are entirely dispensed with; spring contacts on the switch making direct contact with the bulb. Other lamp holders are provided with spring plungers, one end of which presses against the bulb contact, the other being connected to the lead or else to a spring contact on the switch. When cable leads to the lamp interior are used, they may be brought through the base mounting, or through an eyelet in the lamp body, or to an adapter provided so that the leads can be detached without dismantling the lamp.

ELECTRIC LAMPS

Sidecar and Tail Lamps

These are of very simple construction, and do not provide any focusing adjustment. The fronts are detachable so that bulbs may be easily replaced.

Setting

A headlamp should be set to give a horizontal main beam dead ahead or slightly inclined downward and to the left—never upward.

This can be determined by taking the machine on a level road at night, switching on the light, and directing it towards a wall and observing the height of the centre of the beam. Should this be high or low, means are provided in the mounting of the lamp for the adjustment of the setting.

Base-mounted types have a spherical seating which, after the fixing nut has been slackened, permits the lamp to be rocked forward or backward until the correct position is located. A rotary movement of the whole lamp on the stud mounting will enable the forward position of the beam to be accurately fixed.

After adjustment the nut should be carefully tightened or the lamp will quickly shake to pieces.

Fig. 7.—EARLY TYPE LUCAS LAMP DISMANTLED.
In the left hand is the external part of the switch showing the back of the ammeter and the spring blade contacts.

ELECTRIC LAMPS

Side brackets also provide easy adjustment. Slack off the nuts on the side studs, set the lamp position and refix.

Serrated faces or split cones on the brackets and on the washers under the nuts serve to lock the nuts when tightened.

Focusing

To obtain the best results from headlights, the bulb must be accurately focused, i.e. the filament must be as near the focal point of the reflector as possible.

Take the machine on a straight level road at night and adjust the bulb position, with the beam directed on a wall, so that the most brilliant lighting is obtained with a complete absence of black spots, rings or shadows.

The bulbs recommended by the lamp manufacturers should be used, as other types may have the filament in such a position that accurate focusing is impossible.

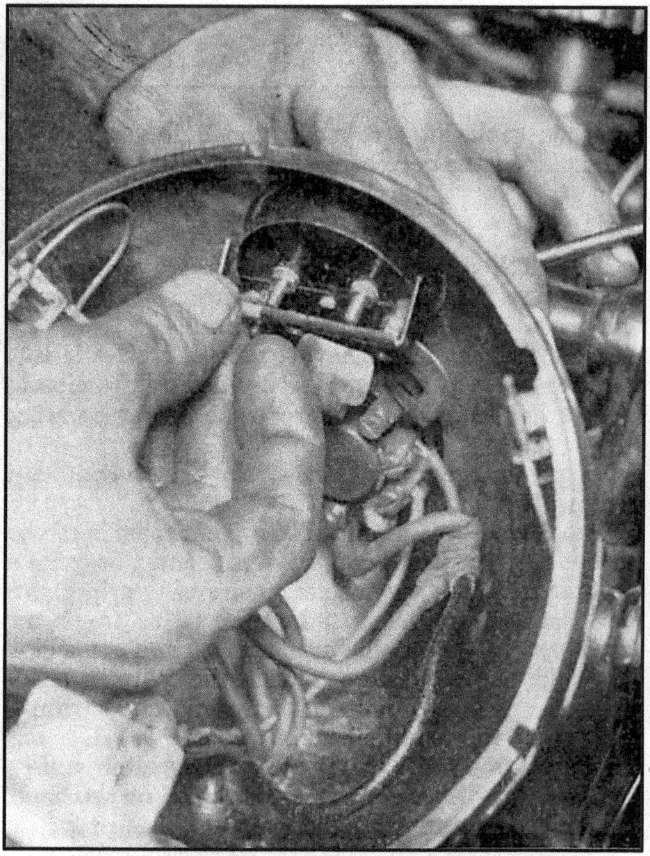

Fig. 8.—FITTING AN AMMETER TO A MILLER LAMP.
A bridge piece is used which takes a bearing on the lamp shell.

Bulbs

When bulbs become old and discoloured, or the filament sags out of position, they should be replaced by new bulbs to ensure good lighting.

When purchasing these it is important to note that the correct voltage, wattage and cap fitting are obtained.

ELECTRIC LAMPS

The following types of lamp bulb are in common use :

Fitting.	B.A.S. No.	Contacts.	Volts.	Watts.	Filament.
S.B.C.	—	Centre	6	6	Single
,,	1	,,	6	12	,,
,,	2	,,	6	18	,,
,,	—	Double	6	18 and 18	Twin
,,	—	,,	6	24 and 24	,,
,,	—	,,	4	12 and 12	,,
,,	B.A.S. 8 S.	Centre	6	3	Single
Screw Cap	—	,,	3·5	·3 amps.	,,

When replacing a dipped beam bulb, care should be taken that the bulb is fitted the correct way round in the holder.

Wiring

The earthed system of wiring is usually adopted for cycle equipments, the positive side only being connected by cables and the frame of the machine used for the negative return.

Two filament bulbs have two positive leads to the bulb holder, and the common return circuit is provided by the metal parts of the lamp, or another lead may be used from the holder or reflector to the frame of the machine.

Single-filament bulbs are of the centre contact type, and have only one lead to the holder.

Good contact is essential between the ends of the cable and the lamp terminals. The bared copper strands must be quite clean, twisted tightly together and fixed by the screw or spring grip provided.

No stray strands must be allowed to touch any other terminal or metal part, and the cable insulation should come close up to the terminal. When the cable is taken outside the lamp, a cord grip, cleat or other means should be provided to prevent any strain on the cable pulling directly on the terminal connections. When a switch is fitted on the lamp, the lamp leads terminate at the switch, unless an extra switch for pilot light or dipping beam is positioned on the handlebars, in which case extra leads are run from the lamp to this switch.

Cleaning

To obtain the maximum efficiency from the lamps, the lenses, reflectors and bulbs should be kept clean.

Reflectors must be handled very carefully. A soft, dry, chamois leather or selvyt cloth should be used, and if the reflector is discoloured a good plate powder or rouge may be sparingly used for polishing purposes. It should be noted that reflectors which are lacquered should not have

ELECTRIC LAMPS

any polishing agent applied, and that a chamois leather only is required to remove finger marks, grease or rain spots, etc. To polish black enamel use a good furniture polish.

LIGHTING FAULTS AND REMEDIES

Fault.—Dirty bulb, lens or reflector.

Symptoms.—Dull or distorted light.

Remedy.—Clean the part affected and replace as necessary.

Fault.—Bulb filament sagged.

Symptoms.—Bulb out of focus. Light poor or distorted.

Remedy.—Renew bulb, adjust focus.

Fault.—Bulb blackened or burnt out.

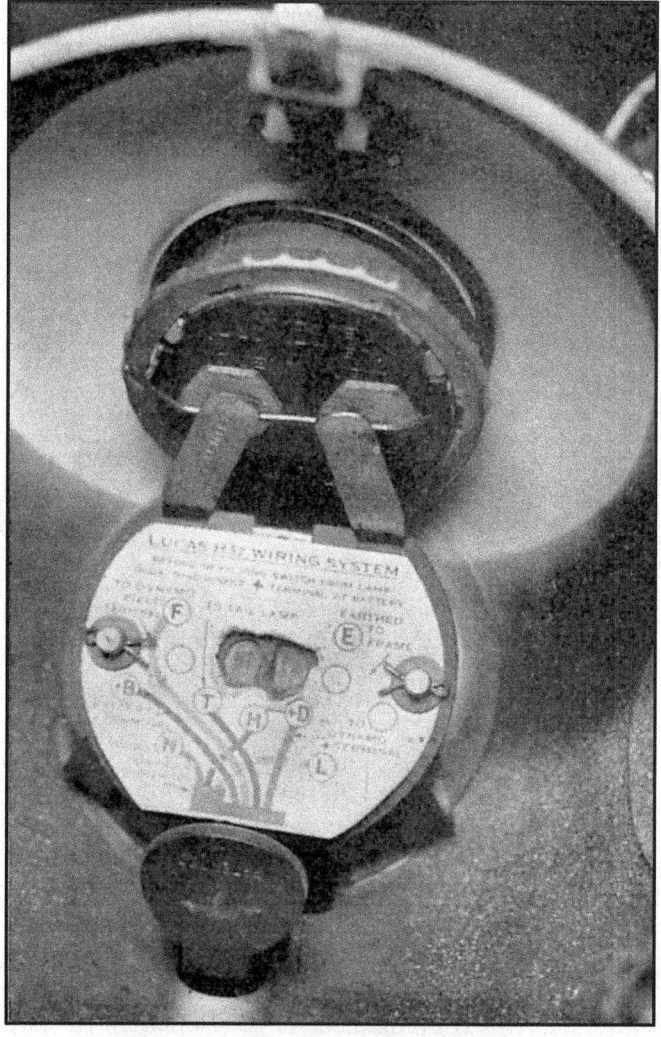

Fig. 9.—An Emergency Lamp Repair.

In the case of a defective ammeter a temporary repair can be made by short circuiting the two terminals with a piece of copper wire as shown.

Symptoms.—Poor or no light. Battery lead broken or loose. Poor earth connection to battery.

Remedy.—Renew bulb and refocus after making good any defect in the battery circuit.

Fault.—Bad earth connection to lamp.

ELECTRIC LAMPS

Symptoms.—Flickering or no light.
Remedy.—Examine earthing wire. Clean terminal ends and tighten connections to frame and lamp.

Fault.—Sticking contact plungers in bulb holder.
Symptoms.—Flickering or no light.
Remedy.—Renew bulb holder. As a temporary repair the plunger can be eased by using a spot of oil on the plunger and working it up and down until free.

Fault.—Defective plunger springs.
Symptoms.—Flickering light.
Remedy.—Renew bulb holder. Sufficiently good contact may be obtained by sweating a spot of solder to the bulb contact or contacts, care being necessary to avoid connecting the bulb contacts to the metal cap of the bulb.

Fault.—Defective contact between switch spring and lamp contacts.
Symptoms.—Flickering light.
Remedy.—Remove switch from lamp and set spring contact forward to increase pressure against bulb. Clean contact surfaces. Renew any broken part.

Fault.—Loose cable lead to bulb holder.
Symptoms.—Flickering or no light. Short circuit on lamp wire.
Remedy.—Remove front and reflector, examine leads to holder and switch and repair as necessary. Tighten terminals and see that contacts are clean.

Fault.—Short circuit on lamp holder.
Symptoms.—Switch contacts or lamp leads burnt.
Remedy.—Remove front and reflector. Test for position of short circuit. Cable ends may be frayed and touching the lamp cap. Plunger spring may be bent and making contact with the cap. The holder insulation may be defective. Spring contact of switch may be bent and touching body of lamp.

Repair as necessary. Test with test lamp and clear the short before reassembling the lamp.

Fault.—Water penetrates into lamp.
Symptoms.—Discoloured reflector. Damaged lens.
Remedy.—Dismantle lamp and clean parts. Renew lens if cracked or broken. Renew rubber ring or defective springs. See that switch is tight on its seating.

Fault.—Loose mounting.
Symptoms.—Lamp rattles. Broken bracket. Broken bulb or leads.
Remedy.—Repair as necessary. Tighten bracket fixing nuts and clamps.

ELECTRIC LAMPS

Fig. 10.—Late Type Lucas Switch Unit.
It is shown withdrawn from the lamp by undoing the two terminals screwed to the studs shown on the lamp. The cables are harnessed together by braiding.

Tail lamps used in conjunction with dry batteries on cycles fitted with flywheel-type generators or other alternate current units have a resistance in series with the bulb when supplied from the generator. If the illumination is insufficient for compliance with recent regulations, it can be increased by cutting down the resistance. The advice of the manufacturers should be asked before doing this.

White enamelling the interior of tail lamps will increase their illuminating capacity.

SWITCHES AND INSTRUMENTS

Types and Operation

Switches are used for controlling the lamp and charge circuits, and may be mounted on the headlamp, on the handlebars, on the tank, or on the frame of the machine.

The usual position is now on the headlamp, and the cut out is mounted directly on the dynamo instead of on the switch box as formerly.

The switch action is generally rotary and the positions OFF—CHARGE—LAMPS are provided on sets including a dynamo.

When a pilot bulb or dim headlight are part of the equipment a further position for " low light " is provided on the switch.

A resistance used for the purpose of reducing the dynamo output when the switch is in the CHARGE position is included in some types of switch.

ELECTRIC LAMPS

On flywheel or other magneto-generator sets the resistance on the switch is used to reduce the voltage on the tail-lamp circuit when fed from the generator, the tail lamp usually having a 3·5-volt bulb so as to be suitable for use with a dry battery.

Battery lighting equipments include a switch having OFF, LOW and HIGH lamp positions.

Flywheel ignition and lighting sets have a switch with OFF—head and tail—and standby light and tail positions.

For dipped beam bulbs a separate switch controls the dipped beam position, and this is usually located on the handlebars.

A panel type of switchboard has recently been introduced, and on this the switch, ammeter, and possibly a speedometer, are mounted. When coil ignition is used, an ignition switch and warning light may be included. This warning light is connected across the dynamo and battery positive terminals when the ignition switch is ON and glows red when the engine is stopped with the switch still on, as a warning that current is being wasted. Should the lamp continue to glow with the engine running at speed, it indicates that the dynamo is not generating for some reason and the cut out has not cut in.

The switch used for dipped beam headlights is a trigger-operated toggle switch, with three terminals for the feed from headlamp terminal on main switch and a lead to each filament contact of the double-filament bulb.

Ammeters

These instruments indicate the amount of charge to or discharge from the battery, and are fitted with those standard equipments which include a dynamo. They are usually mounted on the headlamp casing or in the panel switchboard, and are a very useful guide as to the condition of the dynamo. Some types of ammeter provide for the illumination of the dial by light from one of the headlamp bulbs, the case of the instrument being slotted for this purpose.

The instrument has two terminals, one of which is connected to the battery side of the cut out, and the other to the battery positive. A fixed series coil is connected across the two terminals, in the case of the meter, and a pivoted moving magnet carries the needle indicator, which moves across the centre zero scale of the dial and shows the charge or discharge current in amperes.

SWITCH FAULTS AND REMEDIES

Fault.—Loose connections.

Symptoms.—Light and ammeter needle flickering.

Remedy.—Remove switch. Examine terminals. Adjust cable leads and tighten screws or nuts as necessary.

ELECTRIC LAMPS

Fault.—Loose terminal posts.
Symptoms.—Poor contact. Switch action wedged. Half charge with lamps on.
Remedy.—Readjust and fix terminal posts. If these are moulded into the base, it will be advisable to renew the switch.

Fault.—Switch inoperative.
Symptoms.—No light. Handle loose. Cam or stop plate adrift. Spring plunger contacts jammed.
Remedy.—Dismantle switch. Renew defective spring or plunger. Locate stop and cam in correct position. Reassemble. Tighten terminal screws and handle screw.

Fault.—Burnt contacts.
Symptoms.—Light out or flickering. Broken battery lead.
Remedy.—Repair battery cable. Clean contacts and renew defective parts. A temporary repair may be made by connecting battery lead terminal to the terminal of the lamp circuit required. This temporary connection must be removed at the end of the journey to prevent the battery being discharged.

Fault.—Field contact arm jammed.
Symptoms.—No output in any position.
Remedy.—Remove switch. Free contact arm or lever. Refix with cable clear of contacts.

Fault.—Short-circuited contacts.
Symptoms.—Lights on in OFF or CHARGE positions. Burnt contacts or cable. No light.
Remedy.—Dismantle switch. Examine cable ends for frayed strands. Fix loose contacts. Keep resistance clear of any metal parts except at terminal ends. Renew damaged parts and test out with test lamp.

Fault.—Earthed field connection.
Symptoms.—Full output in CHARGE position. Field lead pinched by fixing screws of switch body.
Remedy.—Remove switch. Repair insulation of lead. Refix, keeping cable clear of fixing screws.

Ammeter Faults

The only faults that can be repaired without expert knowledge are those such as loose terminal connections, which are external to the instrument.

Loose connections are indicated by a flickering needle, overheating of the dynamo and cables.

If after cleaning and tightening the terminal connections the meter is still defective or inoperative, the instrument should be changed. A temporary repair can be made by completely short circuiting the instrument by connecting the two ammeter terminals with a short piece of copper wire of about 16 s.w.g. (Fig. 9).

MOTOR-CYCLE DYNAMOS
INCLUDING NOTES ON CUT OUTS AND REGULATORS

By Edward Hill

Types
  (1) Direct current dynamos.
     (*a*) Concentric—three-brush.
     (*b*) Eccentric—three-brush.
     (*c*) Constant voltage.
  (2) D.C. dynamos combined with magnetos.
     (*a*) Separate units—detachable.
     (*b*) Built in—non-detachable.
  (3) D.C. dynamos combined with distributor or contact breaker for coil ignition sets.
  (4) A.C. generator combined with H.T. ignition unit.
     (*a*) Flywheel type.
     (*b*) Mag-generator type.

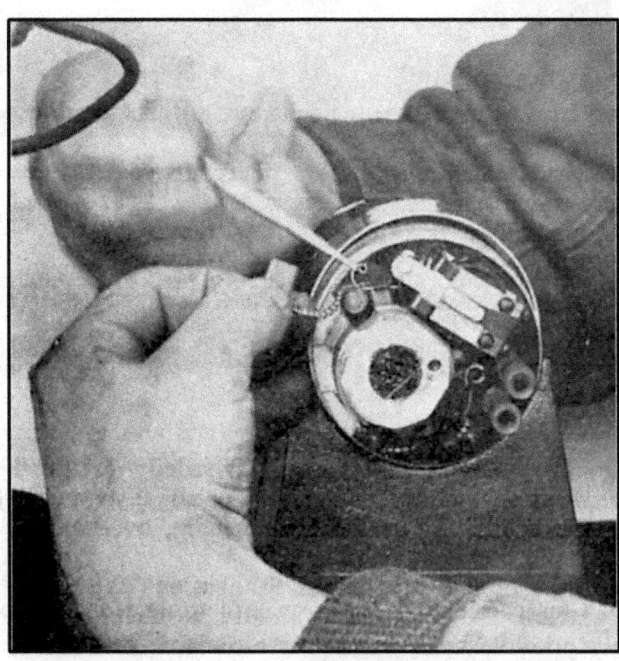

Fig. 1.—Removing Brush from "Miller" S.U.S. Dynamo for Inspection.

The most common type of dynamo is the shunt-wound three-brush constant current type machine driven by belt, chain or gear. Frequently this is combined with the magneto as a detachable or built-in unit, such as the Lucas "Magdyno" and the M.L. "Maglita," which can be treated and described exactly as the separate machines.

These dynamos are generally of the eccentric pattern, having the armature mounted eccentrically in relation to the cylindrical yoke,

DYNAMOS

and being unipolar or more accurately having one wound pole and one consequent pole. This type provides easy adjustment for chain or belt drive by moving the dynamo yoke radially in its saddle mounting.

The general construction of such machines consists of the cylindrical yoke with two end frames carrying the ball bearings of an armature which revolves in the yoke between pole pieces carrying the field windings. The armature windings on the built-up core of the armature are connected to a commutator, and from this the current generated is collected by carbon brushes mounted in holders attached to the end frame. The brushes are pressed against the commutator surface by spring pressure. Terminals for external connections are provided on the commutator end frame and the cut out may also be mounted on the latter. A detachable cover is fixed over this end frame to protect the brush gear and to provide access to the brushes and commutator. Constant current machines must have an accumulator included in the circuit.

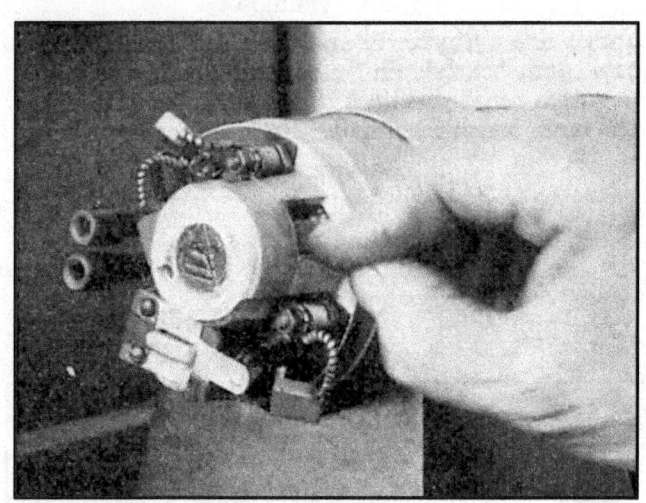

Fig. 2.—Cleaning the Commutator of "Miller" S.U.S. Dynamo.

A small piece of glass paper is applied at the end of the finger through the aperture seen in the commutator and bracket.

In this picture all brushes have been removed for cleaning. Note dynamo plug socket connections. The large hole to be seen in the commutator end bearing casting forms a receptacle into which a small quantity of fairly high melting-point lubricating grease should be pressed from time to time to lubricate the bearing.

Constant voltage machines may be run temporarily with the battery disconnected. Constructionally they are similar to the constant current type except that only two brushes are used, the shunt winding being directly across the two brushes. In addition to a cut out, a regulator is mounted on the machine.

Alternate current machines of the flywheel or mag-generator types are entirely different in construction, and do not employ an accumulator in the circuit. Some form of battery must, however, be used to supply current when standing.

The current generated in the primary circuit of the unit is used to

DYNAMOS

feed the head and tail lights whilst the engine is running. The instructions given for the maintenance and repair of magnetos is applicable to this type of lighting equipment, and are therefore not included in this section.

Regulation

Constant current dynamos have the shunt characteristics modified by some form of regulation *qua* speed, this usually being that known as the "Leitner" or third brush method. The third brush is interposed between the positive and negative brushes, and the shunt field is connected across one main brush and the third brush. Some Lucas dynamos have two main brushes and a control brush, which is connected to the main negative brush terminal. The field circuit in this case is connected across the main brush terminals. In either of these forms the dynamo with this

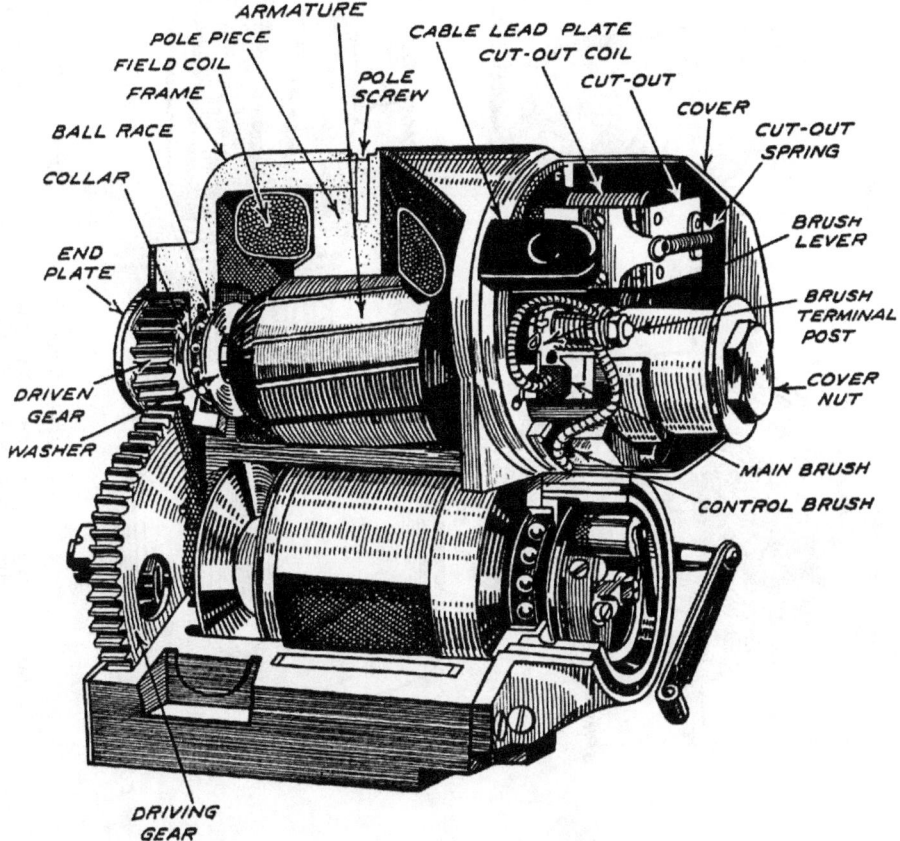

Fig. 3.—"Magdyno," showing the Component Parts.
The dynamo armature can be seen in the upper half of the casing, and the magneto armature below it.

DYNAMOS

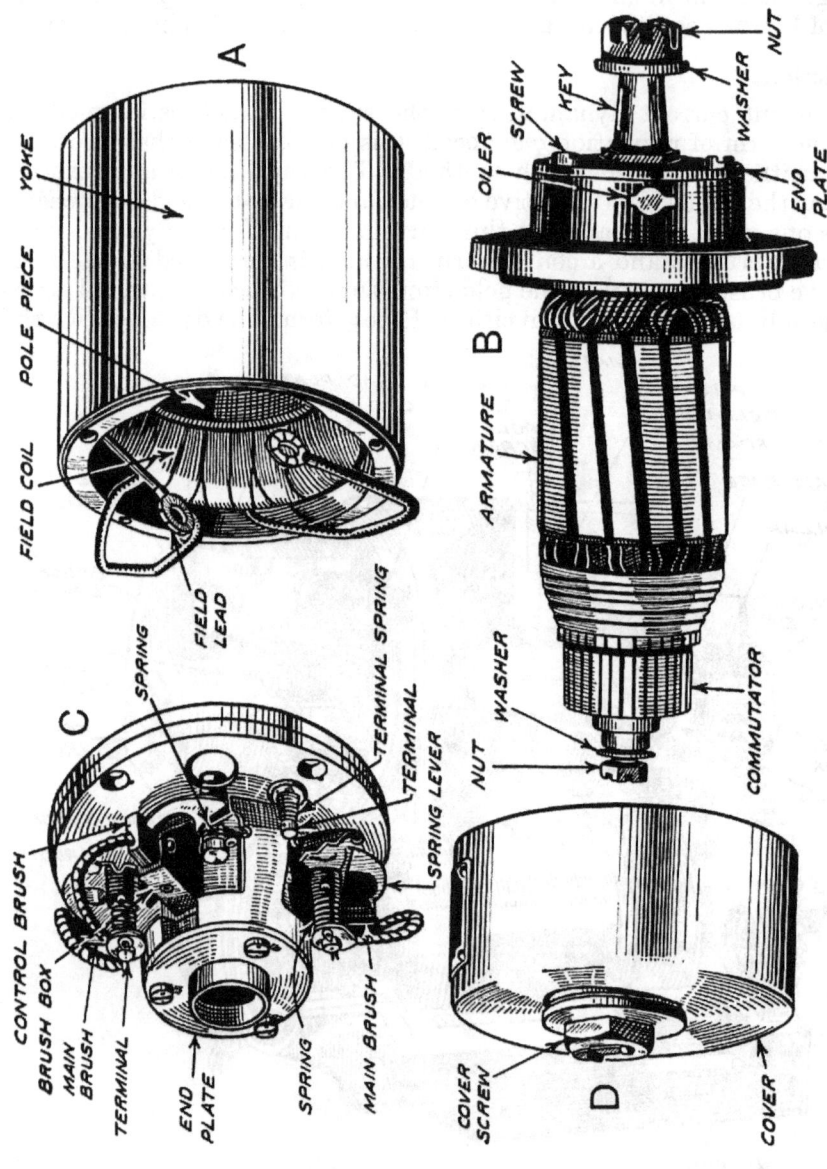

Fig. 4.—A Typical Lighting Dynamo Dismantled.

This shows the chief components very clearly. They are: the magnet frame and field coils, A; the armature assembly, B; the brush gear assembly, C; and the end cover, D.

third brush regulation is capable of generating an approximately constant current over a wide range of speed. When the armature is revolved the voltage builds up rapidly and the cut out cuts in. As speed increases the output quickly attains a peak value, and then gradually tails off owing to the distortion of the magnetic field and by armature reaction, as speed is further increased. A resistance may be connected in series with the field coil circuit for the purpose of reducing the output of the generator. This resistance is short circuited whenever lamps are switched on, so that the full output is then available.

Constant voltage regulation is usually a form of Tyrrell vibrator control which inserts resistance in the field circuit of the dynamo as the voltage of the circuit increases. This regulation controls the voltage independently of load and speed.

Fig. 5.—How to remove a Brush on Lucas "Magdyno." This is done by lifting the spring lever with a small screwdriver and withdrawing the brush. The cut out can also be seen.

Adjustment

Third brush control dynamos may have this brush mounted so as to permit adjustment of the brush position in relation to the main brushes.

DYNAMOS

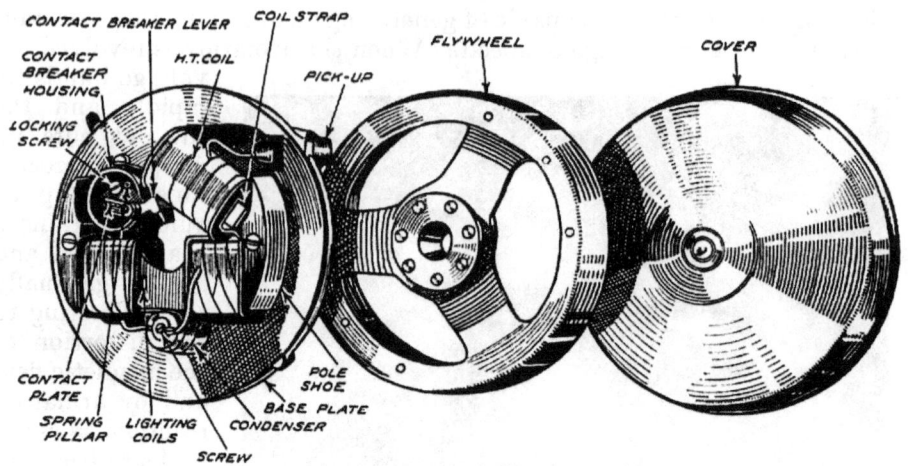

Fig. 6.—A Typical Flywheel Ignition and Lighting Unit.

Movement of the brush in the direction of rotation of the armature will increase the output and vice versa. No adjustment should be made which will increase the output beyond the rated capacity. Should any adjustment be made the brushes must be carefully rebedded, as this may seriously affect the output.

Constant voltage control units are invariably sealed up, and no adjustment beyond the cleaning of contact points is permitted except under the manufacturers' direct instructions.

Maintenance

Before removing the commutator end cover for inspection or other purposes, remove the positive lead of the battery to avoid the possibility of short circuits.

The motor-cycle should not be run with the battery disconnected unless the charge switch is in the OFF position, or damage to the dynamo, cables and bulbs is liable to occur.

Where dynamo is always charging, brushes should be taken from the dynamo.

Inspect the brush gear and commutator periodically. Blow out any carbon dust that may have accumulated—a pair of hand bellows can be usefully employed for this purpose.

The brushes should be a free sliding fit in the holders.

Try this by holding back the spring depression levers and pulling gently on the flexible brush leads. Any tendency to stick should be remedied by cleaning the holder and brush with a cloth moistened with petrol. Overworn or defective brushes should be renewed, and the contact surface carefully bedded to the commutator. A strip of fine glass paper can be

DYNAMOS

used for this purpose, and also, when reversed, for cleaning the commutator.

Use only the make of carbon brush specified by the dynamo manufacturers. Other types may have quite a different wearing effect on the commutator and vary the output by reason of high or low resistance. Test the brush spring tension occasionally. If overheated, these may be softened, and be incapable of pressing the brushes against the commutator with the necessary firmness.

The commutator should be kept free of carbon dust and oil or grease. Remove one of the main brushes and insert in the holder a stick of ebonite or wood covered with a cloth. Press this against the commutator surface whilst revolving the armature.

Clean out the shallow grooves between each commutator section with a knife blade or short piece of hack saw. Smooth off any burrs on the edges or surface of the commutator bars. Clean and tighten all terminal connections and avoid cutting the cable or stripping any screw threads.

The bearings are packed with grease, and do not need attention over long periods, but they should be repacked when the dynamo is dismantled at any time, care being necessary to keep the grease clean and free from grit or metal dust.

On combined magneto and dynamo machines, when the dynamo is gear driven, the gearbox should be opened up and inspected. Examine the gear teeth for wear or breakage.

If the teeth are broken or overworn, the gears should be renewed. The gearbox is packed with grease, and the instructions as for ball bearings should be followed.

Belt or chain drives should be inspected and tightened or adjusted as necessary. Mounting brackets and straps should be examined and the fixing screws tightened.

FAULTS AND REMEDIES

Drive Faults

Fault.—Slipping belt.

Symptoms.—Low output. Flickering ammeter needle. Battery run down.

Remedy.—Clean belt and pulleys. Take up slack. Tighten adjustment fixture.

Fault.—Slack chain.
Symptoms.—Chain runs off. Noisy machine.
Remedy.—Take up slack. Tighten adjustment fixture.

Fault.—Broken belt or chain. Stripped gears. Loose pulley or gear.
Symptoms.—Dynamo idle. Battery run down. Armature may be seized.
Remedy.—Replace or repair belt, chain, gear or pulley as necessary.

DYNAMOS

Remove any cause of dynamo armature seizure, such as worn or dry bearings or loose pole pieces.

Fault.—Loose mounting. Drive out of alignment.
Symptoms.—Noise. Loose belt or chain. Low or intermittent output.
Remedy.—Re-align the setting of the dynamo—the spindle of the dynamo and of the driving wheel must be parallel, and the centres of the pulley grooves or sprocket teeth must be in the same plane. Tighten bracket and strap fixing bolts or clamps.

Brush Gear Faults

Fault.—Brushes broken or overworn.
Symptoms.—Sparking. Overheating. Intermittent output.
Remedy.—Renew brush carbons. Bed new brushes to commutator.

Fault.—Sticking brushes.
Symptoms.—Sparking. Overheating. Intermittent output.
Remedy.—Clean brushes and holders and make carbons free sliding fit in holders.

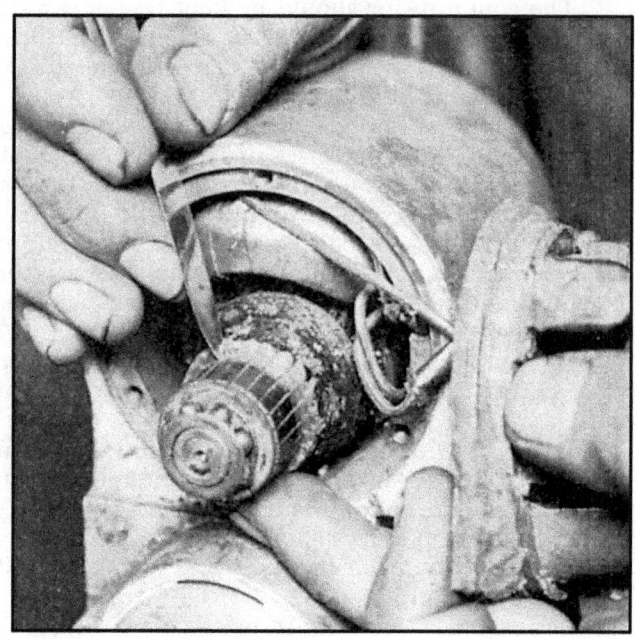

Fig. 7.—CLEANING OUT THE GROOVES BETWEEN THE COMMUTATOR SEGMENTS OF A DYNAMO.
Use a penknife carefully as shown.

Fault.—*Defective or displaced brush springs.*
Symptoms.—Sparking. Overheating. Intermittent output.
Remedy.—Renew defective springs. Adjust lever on top of carbon. Set spring tension to a minimum of $3\frac{1}{2}$ lb. per square inch of brush surface.

Fault.—Broken brush flexibles.
Symptoms.—Low output. Overheated brush gear.
Remedy.—Renew defective brush. Tighten tag screws.

Fault.—Brush holders or flexibles short circuited.
Symptoms.—Dynamo cables and field windings overheated.
Remedy.—Clean brush gear, commutator and end-frame. Note that

DYNAMOS

flexibles are clear of frame, cover and each other, and that commutator is clear of brush holders. Renew damaged parts.

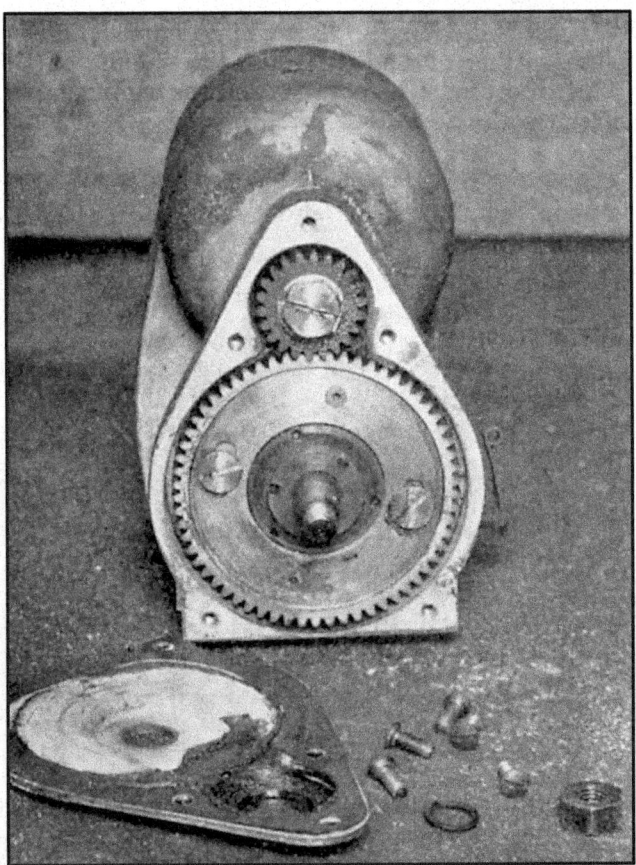

Fig. 8.—Removing "Magdyno" Gear Cover to inspect Pinions and to repack with Grease.
This should be done after every 5,000 miles.

Commutator and Armature Faults

Fault. — Commutator dirty or greasy.
Symptoms.— Low or intermittent output. Sparking.
Remedy. — Blow out carbon dust. Clean commutator, including grooves between segments.

Fault. — Commutator rough or grooved.
Symptoms.— Noisy brushes. Sparking. Flickering ammeter needle.
Remedy. — Smooth and polish commutator with fine glass paper. If the grooves are at all deep, the commutator should be turned true in a lathe. After turning, the insulation between the segments should be undercut.

Fault.—High mica or segment insulation.
Symptoms.—Dynamo will not excite, or output intermittent.
Remedy.—Undercut mica to a depth of $\frac{1}{64}$ inch. Smooth and polish commutator.

Fault.—High commutator bar.
Symptoms.—Noisy brushes. Sparking. Output erratic.

DYNAMOS

Remedy.—Re-turn commutator. If the trouble recurs, the commutator or whole armature should be replaced.

Fault.—Loose connection to commutator.
Symptoms.—Heavy sparking. Intermittent output. Burnt segment.
Remedy.—Resolder faulty joint. Test for earth and continuity and for shorted segments.

Fault.—Loose commutator segments or hub.
Symptoms.—Broken connections to commutator. Severe sparking. Broken brushes.
Remedy.—Commutator must be renewed and reconnected, or whole armature replaced.

Fault.—Earthed or short-circuited commutator.
Symptoms.—Output nil, low or irregular.
Remedy.—Remove armature. Trace fault by means of test lamp and voltage drop test. Clear the defects, or if these persist, renew the armature.

Fault.—Loose armature core.

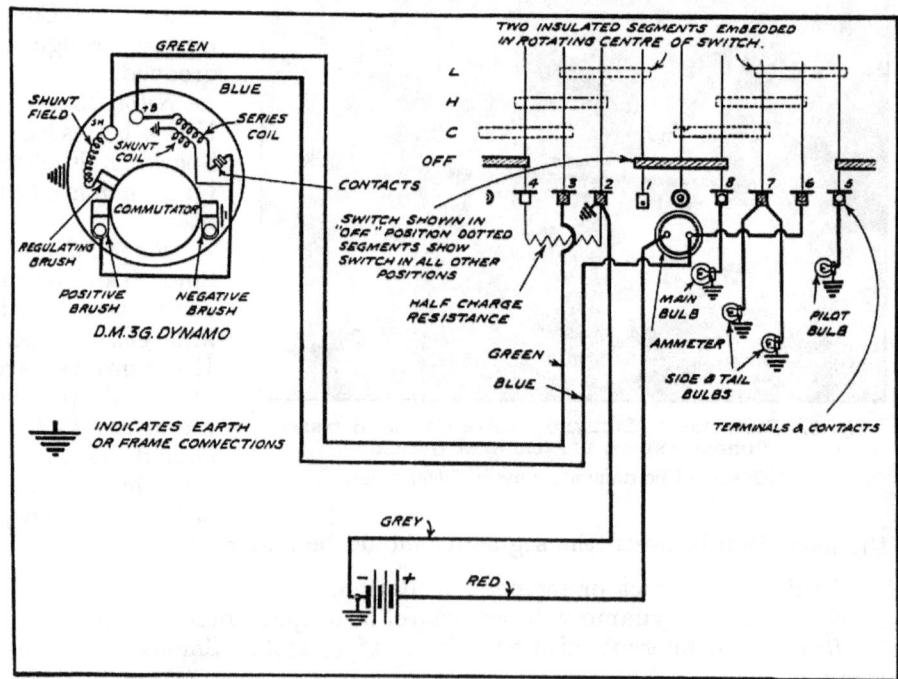

Fig. 9.—The "Miller" Lighting System for Motor-cycles.
The four switch positions are "Off," "Charge," "Half Charge" and "Lights" respectively.

DYNAMOS

Symptoms.—Broken leads between commutator and core. Severe sparking.
Remedy.—Change the armature.

Fault.—Armature fouls pole pieces.
Symptoms.—Noise. Armature seized. Broken banding wires. Loose poles. Worn bearings. Machine overheated.
Remedy.—Dismantle dynamo. Replace or repair damaged parts. Tighten poles hard down. Test armature clearance. If shaft is bent, change the armature.

Fault.—Armature fouls brush gear.
Symptoms.—Severe sparking. Burnt segments and brush holders.
Remedy.—Replace damaged parts. Set brush holders and flexibles clear of commutator. Tighten end-frame screws.

Fault.—Broken banding wires.
Symptoms.—Noisy or seized armature.
Remedy.—Reband armature. Repair or renew damaged coils or leads.

Frame and Coil Defects

Fault.—Loose end frame.
Symptoms.—Noise. Damaged bearings.
Remedy.—Tighten and lock end-frame screws.

Fault.—Break in field circuit.
Symptoms.—Dynamo will not generate.
Remedy.—Set charge switch in ON position. Test coils for continuity, also leads from dynamo to charge switch. Change coil or repair lead as necessary. Tighten terminal screws. Note that brushes are free and springs correctly set.

Fault.—Earthed or short-circuited coil.
Symptoms.—Coils overheated. Output nil or high.
Remedy.—Disconnect coils and test to locate fault. Change defective coil. Strip damaged leads and cover with rubber tape or sleeving.

Fault.—Dynamo depolarised.
Symptoms.—Machine will not excite. Cut out chatters.
Remedy.—Disconnect field leads and re-excite the magnet system by connecting the coils direct to the battery—positive to positive. Run dynamo with field separately excited. Reconnect field to dynamo terminals.

Fault.—Poor " earth " connection.
Symptoms.—Output nil or high. Overheating of wires.
Remedy.—See that dynamo frame makes good metallic contact with saddle or mounting.

Fault.—Loose terminal connections.

DYNAMOS

Symptoms.—As for poor " earth."
Remedy.—Tighten all terminal screws.

Fault.—Broken, worn or " crowded " bearings.
Symptoms.—Noise. Overheating. Armature fouls poles.
Remedy.—Renew defective bearings. Test armature clearances. Repack bearings with grease. Tighten end-frame screws.

Fault.—Dry bearings.
Symptoms.—Overheating. Noise. Seized armature.
Remedy.—Repack bearings with high melting-point grease.

Note.—Should the bearings be of the oilless type, no lubricating oil should be added, as oil will cause the bearings to seize or become stiff.

Dynamos which are oiled up or saturated with water should be completely dismantled, thoroughly cleaned and dried before reassembly. Test for shorts or earths caused by damage to insulation, and renew defective parts.

Fig. 10.—THE CUT OUT ON THE B.T.H. SYSTEM IS SEPARATE AND IS FITTED TO A CONVENIENT PLACE ON THE FRAME.

This shows the cover removed.

Testing the Dynamo

When testing the dynamo particular note should be taken of the following points:

(1) That the battery is in good order, and its connections securely made.
(2) That the earth connections are effective.
(3) That the belt, chain or gear drive is in working order.
(4) That the mounting is secure.

DYNAMOS

(5) That the ammeter reads correctly.

(6) That the switch correctly governs the output in the OFF, CHARGE and LAMP positions.

(7) That the commutator is clean.

(8) That the brushes are well bedded, free in the holders and the spring pressure effective.

(9) That all terminals are tight and clean.

(10) That the cut-out contacts are clean.

Should the dynamo refuse to generate when run, after making the above examination, test for broken leads in the armature, field, cut-out

Fig. 11.—THE CUT OUT ON A LUCAS "MAGDYNO."
The card is held behind the contact points to show irregularities.

and external circuits. Repair as necessary and retest. Test also for short circuits on brush gear, commutator, field coil, cut out, cables and switch, defects in any of which may affect the dynamo output. If it is not possible to effectively repair the fault, do not run the machine except with the switch in the OFF position, i.e. with the field circuit broken, until the dynamo can be taken off and overhauled.

Should it be necessary to use the lamps whilst the dynamo is defective, disconnect the shunt field lead either on the switch or on the dynamo before proceeding to run the machine.

DYNAMOS

When testing the dynamo it should be noted that the reading shown on the ammeter will record the output of the dynamo less any lamp load that may be on, and less any current taken by the coil when coil ignition is used. Therefore a charge reading of 2 amperes charge with a lamp load of 2 amperes and a coil consumption of $1\frac{1}{2}$ amperes will indicate that the dynamo output is $5\frac{1}{2}$ amperes.

A discharge reading of 1 ampere with the same loads will indicate an output of $2\frac{1}{2}$ amperes.

Dynamo Drives

Three forms of drive are in general use—belt, chain and gear. Belt drives usually employ flexible " V " or round leather, and chain drives are generally of the roller chain type. Some tightening arrangement is provided for either of these drives. One method of adjustment utilises the eccentricity of the armature mounting in relation to the magnet frame.

By slackening the strap fixing the dynamo, and partially rotating the yoke in the saddle mounting, the belt or chain drive centres are altered, and can be increased as necessary to tighten the belt or chain. Do not adjust too tightly, especially with a chain drive, or the vibration set up may seriously damage the dynamo.

Gear drives are used on all combined magneto and dynamo units, and transmit the drive from the magneto spindle to the dynamo armature. Steel driving wheels and celeron-driven pinions are used, and the two shafts rotate in opposite directions. In older models an intermediate gear was used, and the direction of rotation was the same for both magnet and dynamo shafts.

Belts

Endless " V " rubber belts are sometimes used, and these can only be tightened by the bracket or dynamo adjustment.

Leather " V " belts, generally known as whittle belts, are made up of leather and steel links, and can be adjusted by taking out a link or substituting a short link for a long one. After removing the screw in the centre of a leather link the leather can be pulled away from the steel pins forming part of the steel links, and the belt opened. A link can then be taken off or added as required.

When a " V " belt is worn at the sides so that it works on the bottom of the pulley grooves, it is necessary to renew the belt. Pulleys and belts should be kept clean and free from grease. When tightening, do not adjust the tension of the belt so strongly as to strain the dynamo spindle or bearings.

Mountings

For separate dynamo units cradle mountings are provided which are bolted to the cycle frame. A steel strap holds the dynamo in place on the cradle.

DYNAMOS

It is essential that the mounting should be rigidly fixed to the frame, and that the dynamo is tightly clamped to the cradle.

The axis of the dynamo must be correctly aligned parallel with the axis of the driving shaft, and the centres of the pulley grooves or sprocket teeth must be in the same plane.

CUT OUTS AND REGULATORS

Cut outs and regulators are usually mounted on the dynamo end frame under the commutator end cover.

A cut out is an automatic switch interposed between the dynamo and battery circuits, which connects the dynamo to the battery when the voltage generated by the dynamo exceeds the voltage of the battery. This unit is not in any sense an overcharge preventer, and cuts out only when the dynamo stops generating or when the voltage of the generator drops sufficiently to allow a discharge of current from the battery through the series coil of the cut out.

Regulators are used on constant voltage sets, and operate in the shunt field circuit of the dynamo. When the voltage of the circuit exceeds a set amount, contacts on the regulator open and insert resistance in the shunt field circuit, thus reducing the output and voltage. Should the voltage continue to rise to a further set value, the shunt field is short circuited, and the output of the dynamo reduced to zero.

The adjustment of cut outs and regulators should be confined to keeping the contacts smooth and clean and to seeing that the terminal connections are tight and making good contact.

Connections

Cut outs have two windings on a central core.

The shunt or fine wire coil is connected across the positive and negative terminals of the dynamo. The series or heavy wire coil has one end connected to the dynamo positive and the other to a terminal on the contact attached to the moving armature. When the cut out operates and cuts in, this contact makes connection with another terminal contact which is connected to the battery positive, so that any current generated by the dynamo passes through the series coil of the cut out to the battery or lamps.

A common terminal suffices for the dynamo positive connection to both cut-out coils. A second terminal is provided for the battery positive, and the shunt coil negative is earthed to the frame.

Faults and Remedies

Fault.—Loose terminal connections.

Symptoms.—Burnt contacts. Output nil or intermittent.

Remedy.—Tighten terminal nuts or screws. If tags are provided see that leads are firmly attached. If unable to fix leads securely by screws or nuts, solder direct to terminal pillar.

Fault.—Break in shunt coil.
Symptoms.—Cut out will not function. No output.
Remedy.—Repair the break if exposed. If break is inside the coil, rewind the coil or renew the cut out. Test for continuity.

Fault.—Break in series coil.
Symptoms.—Burnt contacts. No charge to battery.
Remedy.—As for shunt coil.

Fault.—Burnt contacts.
Symptoms.—Sparking. Chattering. Break in main circuit. Weak spring.
Remedy.—Clean or renew contacts. Test coils. Check spring tension.

Fault.—Defective spring.
Symptoms.—Shunt coil overheated. Sparking and chattering.
Remedy.—Adjust or renew spring. Repair damaged coils and contacts.

Fault.—Cut out sticks in.
Symptoms.—Contacts burnt. Coils overheated. Broken or damaged spring. Battery run down.
Remedy.—Disconnect battery connections as soon as possible, and do not reconnect until fault has been remedied. Repair or renew contacts, coils or spring as necessary. See that armature works freely between its pivots, and that the stop provided to ensure a gap between the magnet core and the armature is effective.

Fault.—Wrong connections to cut out.
Symptoms.—Cut out sticks in. Chattering.
Remedy.—Trace connections through to makers' diagram and reconnect correctly.

A faulty cut out can be temporarily short circuited by connecting the two main terminals of the cut out to the two terminals of a single-pole switch. This switch must only be closed when the dynamo is running above the speed at which the cut out usually cuts in, and must be opened before switching off the engine.

A faulty regulator can be similarly short circuited by connecting the ingoing and outgoing shunt-field leads together by means of a piece of resistance wire—approximately 5 or 6 ohms. of 20 s.w.g. Eureka.

These temporary remedies should only be used as expedients until it is possible to have the cut out or regulator repaired or replaced.

PREVIOUSLY PUBLISHED IN THIS SAME SERIES:

THE BOOK OF 1930's BRITISH MOTORCYCLE GEARBOXES AND CLUTCHES

ISBN: 9781588501813

DESCRIPTION: 108 pages with 112 illustrations packed with hard-to-find detailed information to assist in the overhaul, repair, adjustment and maintenance of pre World War II motorcycle Gearboxes and Clutch systems including:

ALBION: 2 speed Model C, 3 speed Models G, J & E, 4 speed Model H Gearboxes & Clutches.

B.S.A.: 3 & 4 speed Medium & Heavyweight Gearboxes and Light, Medium & Heavyweight Clutches.

BURMAN: 3 & 4 speed Models E. L, R, W, T, M, O & Q.

DOUGLAS: 3 speed Gearbox and A/31 & D/31 type Flywheel Clutches.

NEW HUDSON: Gearbox & Clutch.

RUDGE: 4 Speed Gearbox & Clutch.

SCOTT: 2 & 3 speed Gearbox & Clutch.

STURMEY ARCHER: 3 speed Gearbox plus single spring, multi spring & shock absorber Clutches.

VELOCETTE: Gearbox & Clutches for both 2 stroke & OHC models.

The predominance of the data included in this publication was compiled from 1924-1939 service documentation. However, much of that same information is applicable to motorcycles manufactured before and after those dates. For instance, gearboxes manufactured by Albion, Burman, Sturmey Archer, etc. were installed in a variety of earlier and later motorcycles. In addition, many of the motorcycle manufacturers also utilized their proprietary gearbox and clutch systems in both earlier and later models.

This publication also includes a complete listing of titles in the 'Motorcyclist's Library' series. Many of those books expand on the repair and maintenance procedures for other mechanical and electrical components and will be of assistance to owners and restorers of classic, vintage and veteran motorcycles.

AUTOBOOKS WORKSHOP MANUALS

ALFA ROMEO GIULIA 1300, 1600, 1750, 2000 1962-1978 WSM
BMW 1600 1966-1973 WSM
BMW 2500, 2800, 3.0 & 3.3 1968-1977 WSM
BMW 316, 320, 320i 1975-1977 WSM
BMW 518, 520, 520i 1973-1981 WSM
FIAT 1100, 1100D, 1100R & 1200 1957-1969 WSM
FIAT 124 1966-1974 WSM
FIAT 124 SPORT 1966-1975 WSM
FIAT 125 & 125 SPECIAL 1967-1973 WSM
FIAT 126, 126L, 126 DV, 126/650 & 126/650 DV 1972-1982 WSM
FIAT 127 SALOON, SPECIAL & SPORT, 900, 1050 1971-1981 WSM
FIAT 128 1969-1982 WSM
FIAT 1300, 1500 1961-1967 WSM
FIAT 131 MIRAFIORI 1975-1982 WSM
FIAT 132 1972-1982 WSM
FIAT 500 1957-1973 WSM
FIAT 600, 600D & MULTIPLA 1955-1969 WSM
FIAT 850 1964-1972 WSM
JAGUAR MK 1, 2 1955-1969 WSM
JAGUAR S TYPE, 420 1963-1968 WSM
JAGUAR XK 120, 140, 150 MK 7, 8, 9 1948-1961 WSM
LAND ROVER 1, 2 1948-1961 WSM
MERCEDES-BENZ 190 1959-1968 WSM
MERCEDES-BENZ 220/8 1968-1972 WSM
MERCEDES-BENZ 220B 1959-1965 WSM
MERCEDES-BENZ 230 1963-1968 WSM
MERCEDES-BENZ 250 1968-1972 WSM
MERCEDES-BENZ 280 1968-1972 WSM
MINI 1959-1980 WSM
MORRIS MINOR 1952-1971 WSM
PEUGEOT 404 1960-1975 WSM
PORSCHE 911 1964-1973 WSM
PORSCHE 911 1970-1977 WSM
RENAULT 16 1965-1979 WSM
RENAULT 8, 10, 1100 1962-1971 WSM
ROVER 3500, 3500S 1968-1976 WSM
SUNBEAM RAPIER, ALPINE 1955-1965 WSM
TRIUMPH SPITFIRE, GT6, VITESSE 1962-1968 WSM
TRIUMPH TR4, TR4A 1961-1967 WSM
VOLKSWAGEN BEETLE 1968-1977 WSM

VELOCEPRESS AUTOMOBILE BOOKS & MANUALS

ABARTH BUYERS GUIDE
AUSTIN-HEALEY 6-CYLINDER WSM
AUSTIN-HEALEY SPRITE & MG MIDGET 1958-1971 WSM
BMW 600 LIMOUSINE FACTORY WSM
BMW 600 LIMOUSINE OWNERS HAND BOOK & SERVICE MANUAL
BMW 2000 & 2002 1966-1976 WSM
BMW ISETTA FACTORY WSM
BOOK OF THE CARRERA PANAMERICANA - MEXICAN ROAD RACE
COMPLETE CATALOG OF JAPANESE MOTOR VEHICLES
CORVAIR 1960-1969 OWNERS WORKSHOP MANUAL
CORVETTE V8 1955-1962 OWNERS WORKSHOP MANUAL
DIALED IN - THE JAN OPPERMAN STORY
FERRARI 250/GT SERVICE AND MAINTENANCE
FERRARI 308 SERIES BUYER'S AND OWNER'S GUIDE
FERRARI BERLINETTA LUSSO
FERRARI BROCHURES AND SALES LITERATURE 1946-1967
FERRARI BROCHURES AND SALES LITERATURE 1968-1989
FERRARI GUIDE TO PERFORMANCE
FERRARI OPP, MAINTENANCE & SERVICE H/BOOKS 1948-1963
FERRARI OWNER'S HANDBOOK
FERRARI SERIAL NUMBERS PART I - ODD NUMBERS TO 21399
FERRARI SERIAL NUMBERS PART II - EVEN NUMBERS TO 1050
FERRARI SPYDER CALIFORNIA
FERRARI TUNING TIPS & MAINTENANCE TECHNIQUES
HENRY'S FABULOUS MODEL "A" FORD
HOW TO BUILD A FIBERGLASS CAR
HOW TO BUILD A RACING CAR
HOW TO RESTORE THE MODEL 'A' FORD
IF HEMINGWAY HAD WRITTEN A RACING NOVEL
JAGUAR E-TYPE 3.8 & 4.2 WSM
LE MANS 24 (THE BOOK THAT THE FILM WAS BASED ON)
MASERATI BROCHURES AND SALES LITERATURE
MASERATI OWNER'S HANDBOOK
METROPOLITAN FACTORY WSM
MGA & MGB OWNERS HANDBOOK & WSM
MG MIDGET TC, TD, TF & TF1500 WORKSHOP MANUAL
OBERT'S FIAT GUIDE
PERFORMANCE TUNING THE SUNBEAM TIGER
PORSCHE 356 1948-1965 WSM
PORSCHE 912 WSM
SOUPING THE VOLKSWAGEN
SOLEX CARBURETORS (EMPHASIS ON UK & EU AUTOMOBILES)
SU CARBURETORS (EMPHASIS ON UK AUTOMOBILES)
TRIUMPH TR2, TR3, TR4 1953-1965 WSM
TUNING FOR SPEED (P.E. IRVING)
VEDA ORR'S NEW REVISED HOT ROD PICTORIAL
VOLKSWAGEN TRANSPORTER, TRUCKS, STATION WAGONS WSM
VOLVO 1944-1968 ALL MODELS WSM
WEBER CARBURETORS (EMPHASIS ON ALFA & FIAT)

BROOKLANDS BOOKS & ROAD TEST PORTFOLIOS (RTP)

AC CARS 1904-2009
ALFA ROMEO 1920-1933 ROAD TEST PORTFOLIO
ALFA ROMEO 1934-1940 ROAD TEST PORTFOLIO
BRABHAM RALT HONDA THE RON TAURANAC STORY
BUGATTI TYPE 10 TO TYPE 40 ROAD TEST PORTFOLIO
BUGATTI TYPE 10 TO TYPE 251 ROAD TEST PORTFOLIO
BUGATTI TYPE 41 TO TYPE 55 ROAD TEST PORTFOLIO
BUGATTI TYPE 57 TO TYPE 251 ROAD TEST PORTFOLIO
DELAHAYE ROAD TEST PORTFOLIO
FERRARI ROAD CARS 1946-1956 ROAD TEST PORTFOLIO
FIAT 500 1936-1972 ROAD TEST PORTFOLIO
FIAT DINO ROAD TEST PORTFOLIO
HISPANO SUIZA ROAD TEST PORTFOLIO
HONDA ST1100/ST1300 PAN EUROPEAN 1990-2002 RTP
JAGUAR MK1 & MK2 ROAD TEST PORTFOLIO
LOTUS CORTINA ROAD TEST PORTFOLIO
MV AGUSTA F4 750 & 1000 1997-2007 ROAD TEST PORTFOLIO
TATRA CARS ROAD TEST PORTFOLIO

VELOCEPRESS MOTORCYCLE BOOKS & MANUALS

1930'S BRITISH MOTORCYCLE CARBS & ELEC COMPONENTS (BOOK OF)
1930'S BRITISH MOTORCYCLE GEARBOXES & CLUTCHES (BOOK OF)
AJS SINGLES & TWINS 250cc THRU 1000cc 1932-1948 (BOOK OF)
AJS SINGLES 1955-65 350cc & 500cc (BOOK OF)
AJS SINGLES 1945-60 350cc & 500cc MODELS 16 & 18 (BOOK OF)
ARIEL 1939-1960 4 STROKE SINGLES (BOOK OF)
ARIEL LEADER & ARROW 1958-1964 (BOOK OF)
ARIEL MOTORCYCLES 1933-1951 WSM
ARIEL PREWAR MODELS 1932-1939 (BOOK OF)
BMW M/CYCLES R26 R27 (1955-1967) FACTORY WSM
BMW M/CYCLES R50 R50S R60 R69S (1955-1969) FACTORY WSM
BSA BANTAM ALL MODELS FROM 1948 ONWARDS (BOOK OF)
BSA SINGLES & V-TWINS UP TO 1927 (BOOK OF)
BSA SINGLES & V-TWINS 1936-1939 (BOOK OF)
BSA SINGLES & V-TWINS 1936-1952 (BOOK OF)
BSA OHV & SV SINGLES 250-600cc 1945-1954 (BOOK OF)
BSA OHV & SV SINGLES - 250cc 1954-1970 (BOOK OF)
BSA OHV SINGLES 350 & 500cc 1955-1967 (BOOK OF)
BSA TWINS 1948-1962 (BOOK OF)
BSA TWINS 1962-1969 (SECOND BOOK OF)
CATALOG OF BRITISH MOTORCYCLES (1951 MODELS)
DOUGLAS PRE-WAR ALL MODELS 1929-1939 (BOOK OF)
DOUGLAS POST-WAR ALL MODELS 1948-1957 FACTORY WSM
DUCATI 160cc, 250cc & 350cc OHC MODELS FACTORY WSM
HONDA 50 ALL MODELS UP TO 1970 INC MONKEY & TRAIL (BOOK OF)
HONDA 90 ALL MODELS UP TO 1966 (BOOK OF)
HONDA MOTORCYCLES 125-150 TWINS C/CS/CB/CA WSM
HONDA MOTORCYCLES 250-305 TWINS C/CS/CB WSM
HONDA MOTORCYCLES C100 SUPER CUB WSM
HONDA MOTORCYCLES C110 SPORT CUB 1962-1969 WSM
HONDA TWINS ALL MODELS 50cc THRU 305cc 1960-1966 (BOOK OF)
HONDA TWINS ALL MODELS 125cc THRU 450cc UP TO 1968 (BOOK OF)
INDIAN PONYBIKE, BOY RACER & PAPOOSE ILL PARTS LIST & SALES LIT
J.A.P. ENGINES 1927-1952 & MOTORCYCLES 1934-1952 (BOOK OF)
LAMBRETTA ALL 125 & 150cc MODELS 1947-1957 (BOOK OF)
LAMBRETTA LI & TV MODELS 1957-1970 (SECOND BOOK OF)
MATCHLESS 350 & 500cc SINGLES 1945-1956 (BOOK OF)
MATCHLESS 350 & 500cc SINGLES 1955-1966 (BOOK OF)
MOTORCYCLE ENGINEERING (P. E. Irving)
NORTON 1932-1947 (BOOK OF)
NORTON 1938-1956 (BOOK OF)
NORTON DOMINATOR TWINS 1955-1965 (BOOK OF)
NORTON MODELS 19, 50 & ES2 1955-1963 (BOOK OF)
NORTON MOTORCYCLES 1957-1970 FACTORY WSM
NORTON PREWAR MODELS 1932-1939 (BOOK OF)
NSU PRIMA ALL MODELS 1956-1964 (BOOK OF)
NSU QUICKLY ALL MODELS 1953-1963 (BOOK OF)
RALEIGH MOPEDS 1960-1969 (BOOK OF)
RALEIGH MOTORCYCLES 1919-1933 (BOOK OF)
ROYAL ENFIELD SINGLES & V TWINS 1934-1946 (BOOK OF)
ROYAL ENFIELD SINGLES & V TWINS 1937-1953 (BOOK OF)
ROYAL ENFIELD SINGLES 1946-1962 (BOOK OF)
ROYAL ENFIELD 736cc INTERCEPTOR FACTORY WSM
ROYAL ENFIELD 250cc & 350cc SINGLES 1958-1966 (SECOND BOOK OF)
RUDGE MOTORCYCLES 1933-1939 (BOOK OF)
SPEED AND HOW TO OBTAIN IT
SUNBEAM MOTORCYCLES 1928-1939 (BOOK OF)
SUNBEAM S7 & S8 1946-1957 (BOOK OF)
SUZUKI 50cc & 80cc UP TO 1966 (BOOK OF)
SUZUKI T10 1963-1967 FACTORY WSM
SUZUKI T20 & T200 1965-1969 FACTORY WSM
TRIUMPH PRE-WAR MOTORCYCLE 1935-1939 (BOOK OF)
TRIUMPH MOTORCYCLES 1935-1949 (BOOK OF)
TRIUMPH MOTORCYCLES 1937-1951 WSM
TRIUMPH MOTORCYCLES 1945-1955 FACTORY WSM
TRIUMPH TWINS 1945-1958 (BOOK OF)
TRIUMPH TWINS 1956-1969 (BOOK OF)
VELOCETTE ALL SINGLES & TWINS 1925-1970 (BOOK OF)
VESPA 1951-1961 (BOOK OF)
VESPA 125 & 150cc & GS MODELS 1955-1963 (SECOND BOOK OF)
VESPA 90, 125 & 150cc 1963-1972 (THIRD BOOK OF)
VESPA GS & SS 1955-1968 (BOOK OF)
VILLIERS ENGINE (BOOK OF)
VINCENT MOTORCYCLES 1935-1955 WSM

For a detailed description of any of our titles please visit our website www.VelocePress.com

www.ingramcontent.com/pod-product-compliance
Lightning Source LLC
Chambersburg PA
CBHW070557170426
43201CB00012B/1866